Vierge

Critical Acclaim for Vierge

"In *Vierge*, Rachel skillfully balances the expectation and excitement of adolescence with the danger and reality of what it is to be a young woman. With biting humour and brutal honesty, *Vierge* dives into the complicated and heartbreaking depths of friendship, identity and belonging. Rachel draws you into the play with hijinks and juicy gossip. And then, when you least expect it, hits you with hard truths." —Lisa Codrington, author of *The Adventures of the Black Girl in Her Search for God, Up the Garden Path* and *Cast Iron*

"This is no *Mean Girls* odyssey from clunky to cool for Divine—it's much, much richer than that... Mutombo's skill as a playwright is fiercely evident here, and she's opted for a bold, divisive ending." —Aisling Murphy, *Intermission Magazine*

"Mutombo has great fun creating these characters and having them bicker with and tease each other [...] occasionally hinting at darker, more serious aspects of their lives." —Glen Sumi, *SoSumi*

"Its teenage characters ... feel utterly real, and the things they are contending with – sex, guilt, friendship, and desire in a specific religious and cultural context – are compelling, surprising, funny and emotionally layered. The dialogue crackles, but never condescends." —Quebec Writers Federation Awards Jury

"This play makes one both tear up and laugh out loud, sometimes on the same page..." —Write-on-Q Awards Jury

"A moving exploration of identity, history, community and the spaces in which they unite and invariably push apart, *Vierge* is a memorable baptism into a world beyond the binaries of purity and impurity, Congolese and Canadian, religious and sinful. Mutombo asks us to seek wholeness through fellowship, something which, in itself, may be the most divine thing of all." —Catherine Kustanczy, *Globe and Mail*

Vierge

Rachel Mutombo

Vierge
first published 2025 by Scirocco Drama
An imprint of J. Gordon Shillingford Publishing Inc.

Scirocco Drama Editor: Glenda MacFarlane
Cover design by Doowah Design
Author photo of Rachel Mutombo by Andrew Johnson
Production photos by Dahlia Katz

Printed and bound in Canada on 100% post-consumer recycled paper.

For amateur and professional production rights, please contact:
Playwrights Guild of Canada
info@playwrightsguild.ca
416-703-0201

Library and Archives Canada Cataloguing in Publication

Title: Vierge / Rachel Mutombo.
Names: Mutombo, Rachel, author.
Identifiers: Canadiana 20250259702 | ISBN 9781990738722 (softcover)
Subjects: LCGFT: Drama.
Classification: LCC PS8626.U915 V54 2025 | DDC C812/.6—dc23

We acknowledge the financial support of the Canada Council for the Arts, the Government of Canada, the Manitoba Arts Council, and the Manitoba Government for our publishing program.

J. Gordon Shillingford Publishing
P.O. Box 86, RPO Corydon Avenue, Winnipeg, MB Canada R3M 3S3

Rachel Mutombo

Rachel Mutombo is an award-winning actor and playwright who divides her time between Toronto and Montreal. A graduate of the National Theatre School of Canada's acting program, she has performed in acclaimed productions such as the world premiere of *Selfie* (Young People's Theatre) and the Canadian premiere of *School Girls; Or, the African Mean Girls Play* (Obsidian Theatre / Nightwood Theatre).

As a playwright, Rachel's work has been recognized with multiple awards. *Vierge* won first prize in Infinitheatre's Write-On-Q playwriting competition in 2020 and was shortlisted for the 2024 QWF Prize for Playwriting. Her Theatre for Young Audiences play, *Homeroom,* won the Playwrights Guild of Canada's Tom Hendry Award in 2021. She is also the most recent recipient of the Jon Kaplan Legacy Fund Young Canadian Playwriting Award.

A mentor for Black Theatre Workshop's artist mentorship program and the Paprika Festival, Rachel remains dedicated to supporting emerging voices in the theatre community whenever possible.

Acknowledgements

Thank you to the brilliant actors who showed up with open hearts and minds to support the development of this play at every stage: Yvonne Addai, Akosua Amo-Adem, JD Leslie, Seeara Lindsay, Bria Mclaughlin, Joy Mwandemange, Nicole Nwokolo, Khadijha Roberts-Abdullah, Kudakwashe Rutendo, Espoir Segbeaya, Symantha Stewart, Meghan Swaby, and Shauna Thompson.

Thank you to Nina Lee Aquino for being a champion for me and this story from day one. My gratitude knows no bounds.

Thank you, Matt McGeachy, for your gift of dramaturgy.

Thank you to Dian Marie Bridge and Sarah Kitz and the teams at Black Theatre Workshop and Great Canadian Theatre Company, respectively, for giving this play a second life—a critical piece of the development process, but a privilege that is not accorded to every new play.

Playwright's Note

"My name is Divine Ntumba Kabamba, like could I be any more Congolese?"

Without fail, every time I hear this line, I laugh. Divine's need to convince the other girls in the room that she *is*, in fact, Congolese is funny to me. But it's also a little sad. That she feels the need to convince them, despite the blood coursing through her veins, despite who raised her—says something. She tells herself they need convincing. Because she does.

I, too, have a very Congolese full name. However, the experience of growing up in a country where my names have been mispronounced into oblivion or distorted into a punchline has made for a complicated relationship.

Rachel is a common first name, and for that, I have always thanked my parents. As much as possible, I avoid mentioning my middle name—to make it easier. That's what I tell myself. And at times, it's like I forget it's supposed to be there.

But my middle name means so much. Many of my cousins and one of my nieces also share this middle name. We are named after my maternal grandmother, who was a tender and tenacious woman and the anchor of my mom's side of the family. Names—the ones we were given or the ones we have chosen—are so important. In mine, there is a legacy of powerful, beautiful Congolese women who I love dearly. And in neglecting my full name, I lost sight of that.

I wrote this play to celebrate and honour the resilience, courage, and hilarity of African women. With this play, I embrace who I am. I embrace who I've always been—no convincing needed. I celebrate my people, the various communities I belong to, and all our complexities. I'm grateful to invite you into this world. A world that is as restrictive as it is expressive. A world that reminds us of the beauty and absurdity of being a teenager: the triviality and the significance of it all.

And I invite you to remember that laughter and tears are two sides of the same coin.

Rachel Yowa Mutombo
Montreal, QC

Foreword

For many immigrants, the church serves as a sanctuary—a sacred safe space carved out in an unfamiliar country. In a sense, it becomes a home a million miles away from home. It's a place where one can worship in their native tongue, savour the flavours of food from their childhood, and nurture the strength of a shared community. Yet, while the church offers solace, it also reveals the danger of stagnation. In clinging to what is familiar, does it inadvertently blind itself to the truth and realities of the outside world?

This tension forms the backdrop of Rachel's remarkable play. She deftly navigates the generational divide between the steadfast older generation, anchored in tradition—for better or for worse—and the younger generation, boldly stepping into a world that feels more thrilling than daunting. It is within this gap, this push and pull between holding on and letting go, where the truth of this story lives.

When I directed the world premiere of this play, the central question for me was: How can a young woman break free from the weight of cultural expectations to access a different kind of sanctuary—one that actually brings her closer to the divine, to a beauty that is undeniable and true—when that access is only made possible through the confines of a community, through the hands of men?

It is undeniable the amount of power men hold in the African church. To discount or even hold them accountable requires a reckoning of the very foundation of a culture that's been built with them at the centre. And for many within this community, to break this traditional anchor a million miles away from home could disrupt the order of this "well" constructed sanctuary.

And if this community fractures, what will they have left to lean on? So, in the too familiar cases of sexual abuse in the church, is it not easier to tuck away all the discretions and simply assume that, like women before them have, these young women should shut their mouths and swallow the pain in order to preserve the same system that degrades them? Is that not what it means to be faithful to the church? To God?

The existence of this play, unequivocally, says no. And with every turn of each of these pages our playwright fights against this continually false and abusive narrative. It is in the unravelling of the hypocrisy of these beliefs where the potency of this play thrives.

In fact, I've come to realize that the answer to my central question lies in the very publication of this play. Rachel fearlessly exposes the true cost of the negligence of parents and leaders, and the perpetual violence that will not stop unless it is confronted. What better way to do that than to tell the truth, shame the devil, and place four darkskinned women on stage, in front of thousands of people, centering their authentic experience—flaws and all? This is the true magic of *Vierge*—this story belongs to no one but these young women. This is their moment to take centre stage in a space that has continually silenced them.

This is what excites me as a fellow African artist, to get to witness a brave, hilarious, and—most importantly—authentic depiction of our stories in an industry that lives in a single narrative of our realities. I could not be prouder of this moment of publication and to get to have the privilege of being a part of this play's history. It is time for this kind of work that is written by Africans and for Africans to be published, produced and celebrated on a global scale.

This is just the beginning.

Natasha Mumba
Toronto, ON

Natasha Mumba is a Zambian-Canadian actor and director currently based in Toronto.

Production History

The world premiere of *Vierge* was produced by Factory Theatre in Toronto, Ontario from April 8 to 30, 2023, with the following cast and creative team:

Cast

Divine Kabamba: .... Shauna Thompson
Grace Katende: .... Yvonne Addai
Sarah Katende: .... JD Leslie
Bien-Aimé Ilunga: .... Kudakwashe Rutendo

Creative Team

Director: .... Natasha Mumba
Dramaturge: .... Matt McGeachy
Assistant Director &
Movement Director: .... Virgilia Griffith
Stage Manager: .... Ada Aguilar
Assistant Stage Manager: .... Anna Spencer
Set and Props Design: .... Rachel Forbes
Costume Design: .... Joyce Padua
Lighting Design: .... Jareth Li
Sound Design: .... Andrew Johnson

Divine (Shauna Thompson) daydreams sharing her baptism speech to the congregation. Photo by Dahlia Katz.

Divine (Shauna Thompson) and Bien-Aimé (Kudakwashe Rutendo) pray as Grace (Yvonne Addai) and Sarah (JD Leslie) act up. Photo by Dahlia Katz.

Characters

Divine Kabamba:	Sixteen years old, optimistic, honest, enthusiastic about Christ
Grace Katende:	Seventeen years old, sensitive, intelligent, resolute
Sarah Katende:	Seventeen years old, protective, sharp, brave
Bien-Aimé Ilunga:	Seventeen years old, cunning, bright, wise beyond her years

Setting

This play is set in the basement of L'Église du Seigneur, a fictional Pentecostal Congolese church in Montreal, Canada. This is a small church of a multilingual immigrant community where everyone knows everyone.

Any mention of Congo in this play is a reference to The Democratic Republic of Congo (former Zaire).

Notes on the Text

Slashes *(/)* in a line indicate where the next character's line should begin.

Beat is a silent moment of action that indicates a shift for all the characters in the scene. When the *(Beat.)* is in dialogue, the shift is only for that character.

Notes on Production

All the characters in this play are Congolese. These roles are to be played by actors of African descent. The characters of Grace and Sarah speak English with a Congolese accent.

As needed, the mention of "Ebola" in scene two can be changed to "monkeypox." In scene six, the mention of "Photoshop" can be changed to "AI."

Scene One

Lights up on the basement of a Pentecostal Congolese Church, L'Église du Seigneur. One of the ceiling lights flickers, struggling to stay turned on. This basement hasn't been occupied for some time. There are no windows, no daylight—we can only assume the time of day.

And then there was light. A young girl, sixteen, eagerly comes down the stairs, clutching a Bible to her chest. She pulls down the sleeve of her shirt and wipes down the table. She places her Bible on it. She grabs a few foldable chairs and places them around the table. She sits at the head of the table. Decides against it and sits on the far end. She takes in the space, laces her fingers together, closes her eyes and bows her head.

DIVINE: Heavenly Father, thank you for guiding me through every moment of this day. Thank you for your protection and your endless love. Thank you for all the young believers who will join me tonight for this first small group meeting. Lord, may the Holy Spirit fill this space with peace as all of us young women get to know each other. Fill our conversations with your wisdom and truth. Open our hearts to your word... and to each other...God, I don't know if you want us to be friends, but I would really like that—that your—

She is interrupted by laughter. Two more young girls have entered the basement together.

GRACE: Are you praying for friendship?

SARAH: Wow.

DIVINE: No, I was—

GRACE: God answered your prayers, here I am.

SARAH: I am here too.

DIVINE: Okay... Hi, I'm Divine.

DIVINE extends her hand, GRACE dismisses it. SARAH shakes it.

GRACE: Tu rigoles? *(Are you kidding?)*

DIVINE: No, that's seriously my name. What are your—

GRACE: Are you baptized?

DIVINE: Not yet. Are you?

SARAH: Of course.

GRACE: What are you waiting for?

DIVINE: Nothing. I mean I'm just—there's a baptism ceremony on Easter weekend—which you probably know—I'm hoping to do it then. It's right near my birthday so the timing is pretty / perfect…

SARAH: How old are you going to be—

GRACE: I'm Grace, by the way. This is Sarah—

SARAH: We are sisters.

DIVINE: Oh! You look alike.

Beat.

GRACE: When is your birth date exactly?

DIVINE: April 16th.

GRACE: Hm. An emotional Aries, eh?

DIVINE: Oh—I don't really— I don't know much about astrology—

SARAH: Eh! Astrology. Sorcellerie. *(Witchcraft.)*

GRACE: Oh please, they only call the fun stuff witchcraft.

SARAH: Only fun until Satan comes to collect your soul.

DIVINE: So how long—

GRACE: Is it just us three?

DIVINE: No no, Pasteur Ben's email said to expect there to be at least six girls in total for tonight. Hopefully moving forward more girls will join!

GRACE: You really live for Jesus, don't you?

DIVINE: Isn't that the point?

GRACE: You and Pasteur Ben email a lot?

DIVINE: Not really, just when—

SARAH: You know his wife died, right?

DIVINE: Yes, I saw the memorial in—

GRACE: Her name was Mama Jackie.

DIVINE: Right, I—

GRACE: I was at the funeral.

SARAH: Tantine Rose Tshibangu said that Mama Jackie was pregnant when she died.

DIVINE: How does Tantine—

GRACE: With twins, she said.

SARAH: And they had fertility problems for YEARS before so it is more tragic.

DIVINE: Why would she tell you—

SARAH: Tantine Rose is our papa's brother's new wife. She was talking about it with Papa, because she works at the hospital where the pastor's wife died. So it is fact.

DIVINE: Wow, that's really sad… May God be with / Pasteur Ben in his—

GRACE: Now that the lead pastor is a widow, all the single women in the church have become hyenas. Laughing at all his jokes, drooling when he walks by, showing up at his house with plates of food and condolences.

SARAH: Especially the ones over the age of thirty. You can smell their desire in any room.

GRACE: I get it, Pasteur Ben is pretty sexy.

DIVINE: Oh! I—I don't—do you think we should talk about a man of God like that?

SARAH: Why not if it's true?

GRACE: God made him in His image.

GRACE and SARAH cackle.

DIVINE: Pasteur Ben—the email mentioned that you both are new to Canada, right?

GRACE: Mhm. Isn't my English excellent?

SARAH: Papa bought us all these CDs to learn as soon as we knew we were going to move to North America.

GRACE: The lady on the CD was British. I decided not to do her British accent when I learned English because I wanted Canadians to accept me.

DIVINE: Yeah, your English is great.

GRACE: I know.

DIVINE: When did your family arrive?

GRACE: My parents and I have been here since August. Sarah just arrived before Christmas.

DIVINE: Wow, you must have had such a culture shock.

SARAH: A what?

DIVINE: Sorry, that might be a bit of a colloquialism. I just mean you must have been shocked when you arrived in Canada. Especially, in Quebec, with the winter—

GRACE: Eh… It's Congo, not Jupiter. We understand your colloquolo. You just don't speak clearly sometimes. C'est tout. *(That's it.)*

SARAH: Anyway, it's not a shock, really. We have a lot of mundele *(White people)* in Kinshasa.

DIVINE: I'm sorry if I—I just meant it snows a lot here. And like I know I would be shocked if I ever went to Congo.

SARAH: You've never been?!

DIVINE shakes her head no.

GRACE: Obviously. She's a mundele herself.

DIVINE: Sorry… I don't speak Lingala. What does mundele mean?

Beat.

SARAH: White person.

DIVINE reaches for her Bible.

DIVINE: I'm not sure where the other girls are, so maybe we can just start.

She realizes the other girls didn't bring Bibles.

DIVINE: Oh, I guess we can share…

SARAH: To be honest—

GRACE: The Bible is kind of boring.

SARAH: Yeah, just sin, sin, plague, manna, death, sin… boring.

GRACE: The miracles are cool. Turning water into wine.

SARAH: Yes, there should be more turning water into wine in the Bible.

GRACE: Oh! And in life!

DIVINE: Do you… uhm—you drink?

SARAH: You don't?

DIVINE: Well, no, I'm only sixteen.

They burst out laughing.

GRACE: Oh, mundele girl, you have so much to learn yet.

DIVINE: Could you just call me Divine? Please.

GRACE: It's a joke.

SARAH: A cute name. Uhm—nickname? Right?

DIVINE: Right…

GRACE: Yes, mundele girl. Cute nickname. Because you are so cute.

DIVINE: What are your nicknames?

GRACE: So. Is anyone else joining us or what? Sad youth group with only three youths.

SARAH: Yeah, where are the boys?

DIVINE: Pasteur Ben prefers to keep us separate from the boys at this point. Because of—

GRACE: Because of what happened to Ya Elize?

SARAH: Mhm… Tantine Rose Tshibangu said she is to have a baby girl. Funny, eh? From Bible camp to motherhood. Jesus.

GRACE: Jesus bless her.

DIVINE: Jesus bless her. That's why this small group is so important. That we as young women support and uplift each other in our chastity. And when the time / comes to be courted that we—

SARAH: Chasti—what?

DIVINE: Chasteté? *(Chastity?)* To be chaste—to abstain from… you know…uh… / to not… engage in…. to….

GRACE: Eh eh, Divine, qu'est-ce qui se passe? *(What is going on?)*

SARAH: I think she's broken.

DIVINE: Sorry, no. I just—I—

GRACE: Okay, so the only naked boys you have seen are through a computer screen.

DIVINE: What? No! I don't—consuming pornographic images corrupts the mind and softens our hearts towards sin.

GRACE: No, it does not.

SARAH: They are just nice to look at, even better when it's real life.

GRACE: Mhm in 3-D, and you can touch them.

SARAH: ...or lick them.

DIVINE is wildly uncomfortable. GRACE and SARAH burst out laughing.

We are joking, petite soeur *(little sister)*. We are chaste. Saved. Holy.

GRACE: Virgins... with a few exceptions.

DIVINE: Exceptions?

GRACE: Like a vegetarian who sometimes eats fish.

DIVINE: Pescatarian?

GRACE: A what?

SARAH: Like a vegetarian who eats a steak, but does not finish it.

DIVINE: So you start—it... but don't finish?

GRACE: Something like that.

DIVINE: Like the bases?

SARAH: Bases?

GRACE: Bases?

DIVINE: Yes, like in baseball. First base, second base, third base…

SARAH: Home run!

GRACE: Yes, mundele girl, look at you. You are getting it.

DIVINE: No, no, I'm not, I'm just trying to— But isn't that still kind of a sin?

SARAH: Mundele, we are supposed to sin!

DIVINE: I mean, we all sin, but I don't think we're supposed to—

GRACE: Ahhh, when Adam and Eve ate the apple they didn't die. Right?

DIVINE: It wasn't an apple. Just a fruit—

GRACE: Right. Just a punishment.

DIVINE: …they were banished from the Garden of Eden and sentenced to a life of pain / but okay…

GRACE: Exact! God loves us, hmm? He sent his one and only son to die on the cross for all our sins and whatever!

SARAH: So we have to sin! We can't let Jesus sacrifice go to waste—

DIVINE: I don't think—

GRACE: Plus, the Bible and all the translations: Hebrew, Greek, English, French, Lingala… oof, c'est compliqué. *(it's complicated.)*

Quietly, another young woman floats into the room. She has a bag slung over her shoulder. A Bible casually held in one of her hands.

BIEN-AIMÉ: So I'm a little late and still no Bibles are open?

SARAH: A little late?

DIVINE: You must be running on African time.

DIVINE laughs at her joke, the others do not.

GRACE: Eh, that's an offence to us.

SARAH: Yeah, not all Africans are the same.

DIVINE: Sorry, it was a—I mean, you were all late tonight so... *(Beat.)* Uhm, do you three already know each other?

BIEN-AIMÉ: Unfortunately.

GRACE lets out an overenthusiastic laugh. BIEN-AIMÉ greets GRACE with the traditional three cheek kisses. DIVINE watches curiously, trying to catch on to the tradition.

I'm Bien-Aimé.

DIVINE: Divine.

BIEN-AIMÉ: Oh! So how did the gift from God herself end up leading this group of heathens?

GRACE: Yeah, where did you come from anyway?

DIVINE: Canada. Uh—you mean like where did I come from today? Or originally? Or—I—I'm / sorry, I don't know what you mean?

BIEN-AIMÉ: You're new to the church?

DIVINE: Right. Yes. Since the New Year. My family used to go to Roxboro Faith. I was part of a young women's small group, we used to do weekly Bible study and—so I was looking forward to joining one when my family came to L'Église du Seigneur, but there weren't any yet. So I asked Pasteur Ben about it after a Sunday service and kinda sorta volunteered myself for it? To lead the group. Well, actually at Roxboro Faith small groups don't have a leader, it's a collaborative—

BIEN-AIMÉ: Wait, hold on. You went to Roxboro Faith? Isn't that a White People church?

DIVINE: Well, the pastors were White, but the congregation was mixed—diverse? They—they had people of lots of different ethnicities.

BIEN-AIMÉ: Hmph… *(Beat.)* So what brings you to L'Église?

DIVINE: My parents are Congolese—uh, well, I am too. Obviously. Right, uh, yeah… my parents wanted to come here. I'm happy to be here too, I just didn't choose it—well, church is church no matter— "Where two or three are gathered in His name, He is in the midst / of them…"

SARAH: Do White people sing in their churches?

DIVINE: Of course, worship is worship regardless of race.

GRACE: They sing to organ music with serious faces. They don't know how to worship Jesus with their whole bodies like Africans.

SARAH whips out her phone, plays a worship song in Lingala and immediately she and GRACE are on their feet dancing with vigour. The dancing begins to get increasingly more inappropriate, BIEN-AIMÉ joins in, stealing their spotlight. DIVINE watches in a mixture of shock and interest. She wants to stop them but also can't look away. They are free and happy, comfortable in their bodies. BIEN-AIMÉ notices DIVINE and pulls her on to her feet. She resists a bit, BIEN-AIMÉ insists and gets her moving. DIVINE is awkward, slightly off beat but she's having fun. GRACE is twerking and gyrating all over the basement at this point. SARAH fights to keep up, even breaking a sweat.

SARAH: I want to see you really move, Mundele!

GRACE: Dance with us! Feel the afro-beats in your blood.

DIVINE snaps out of it.

DIVINE: Okay! That was fun.

They ignore her.

Maybe we can turn to the Book of Ruth, Chapter 1...

The other girls continue to dance. DIVINE rushes to the phone and stops the music.

We're in God's house. We shouldn't be dancing like the Israelites before the golden calf.

SARAH and GRACE groan.

BIEN-AIMÉ: Psalm 149:3 "Let them praise His name with dancing; Let them sing praises to Him with timbrel and harp." Dancing is worshipping God. They didn't tell you that at Roxboro Faith?

GRACE snickers, SARAH joins in.

GRACE: Elle croit qu'elle est meilleure que nous. *(She thinks she's better than us.)*

SARAH: Tellement fière. *(So proud.)*

DIVINE: Non, pas du tout—*(No, not at all—)*

GRACE: Yes! Since we walked in tonight you have been treating us like aliens because we just immigrated. Just because we've never seen snow or whatever.

SARAH: Just like the Canadians. They don't know better. But you are worse than them. You're supposed to be one of us.

DIVINE: No, I'm not. I mean—I am one of you. My name is Divine Ntumba Kabamba, like could I be any more Congolese? *(Beat.)* I don't mean to be judgy, I'm just— The girls at Roxboro are nothing like any of you. They'd probably pass out if they saw the way you worship— Sorry, I— I think you're all pretty great…so far. And and and you speak Lingala and it's so easy for you to— you're like real Africans. Like from Congo—unlike me… you know. Mundele girl…. So… maybe I'm not the right person to lead this small group? I don't want anyone feeling uncomfortable or maybe I need to just take a backseat for a second, I know I just got here—I kinda got excited… I'm sorry, I don't / really know what I'm—

BIEN-AIMÉ: Not even one full session of this small group and we already have this poor girl ready to quit.

GRACE: You might not be cut out for it, Mundele.

DIVINE: No, maybe I'm not—

BIEN-AIMÉ: Don't give up on us just yet. Didn't Jesus say that thing about not judging people or whatever? So, who are we to judge you? Most Africans barely like each other as it is. When my mom found out I was dating a Muluba boy, she started talking about how people from that tribe are controlling and aggressive and—pfft, at least he's from Congo! Imagine if I brought home a Nigerian.

GRACE and SARAH cackle.

Eh! I'd never hear the end of it.

DIVINE: ...You have a boyfriend?

BIEN-AIMÉ: Yep. He comes to church here too.

GRACE: Eric Mwanza.

BIEN-AIMÉ whips out her phone to show DIVINE her background photo. GRACE peeks.

192 centimetres of chocolate goodness.

DIVINE: Oh. Wow. He's—wow. Congratulations.

BIEN-AIMÉ: Ohh, another one who is interested in my man.

DIVINE: What? No—I—

SARAH: Mhm, so she does like men after all. I was beginning to wonder if you were spinning the other way.

DIVINE: Swing. The other way.

GRACE: Do you?

DIVINE: No. That's—

SARAH: A sin, yeah, yeah, we know.

BIEN-AIMÉ: I know I know, I am incredibly blessed.

GRACE: Praise God.

BIEN-AIMÉ: Eric is different. But most guys that look like him are easy enough to get. It's a matter of knowing how to keep them.

DIVINE: ...How?

GRACE and SARAH make overt blowjob gestures with their mouths and hands.

You're not—you mean in your mouth?

BIEN-AIMÉ: That's usually the easiest option if you're trying to stay a virgin.

GRACE: Eh eh, Divine, close your mouth or you'll swallow a fly.

SARAH: Do you need water?

DIVINE: No. No, I'm... tonight has gone differently than I expected. I expected prayer, and worship and sisterhood and... Bible, a lot more Bible.

GRACE: We worshipped.

SARAH: Oh yeah.

SARAH twerks.

BIEN-AIMÉ: And here's your sisterhood.

DIVINE: But I'm supposed to make sure we get through the book of Ruth over the next few weeks, and Pasteur Ben—

GRACE: You know that's why nobody else came.

DIVINE: What do you mean?

GRACE: That boring email about taking "a deep dive through the waters of the book of Ruth…"

SARAH: "…maintaining our purity as Sisters in Christ."

DIVINE: If it was so boring, why are you here?

SARAH: Papa made us.

GRACE: Papa made us.

DIVINE: Oh.

GRACE: It's okay to be boring. Now less girls showed up, so this is more excluded.

BIEN-AIMÉ: Exclusive.

GRACE: Mhm, merci. *(thank you.)*

BIEN-AIMÉ: She's right, though. Less girls, more bonding. Besides, I barely get to see Grace anymore—ever since Sarah landed and stole her away.

GRACE: She didn't….

SARAH: I'm her sister.

BIEN-AIMÉ: Yes yes, you keep reminding everyone of that.

DIVINE: So was my email really that bad? Maybe I can send out another and—

BIEN-AIMÉ: No way. Their loss. Also, ma chérie, you're not hearing us. Your emails are boring. The only person they inspire is Pasteur Ben and well…

DIVINE: And..?

BIEN-AIMÉ: He's depressed and weird.

DIVINE: His wife died.

BIEN-AIMÉ: So he should go on antidepressants like everyone else. But his weird, mopey face every Sunday is a vibe killer… just saying.

SARAH: Or maybe you are jealous.

BIEN-AIMÉ: Excuse me?

SARAH: Pasteur Ben has all the women in the church floating around him now. A pack of gazelles desperate to be devoured by a depressed lion.

BIEN-AIMÉ: What does that have to do with me?

SARAH: Nothing.

BIEN-AIMÉ: Did you knock your big head during some turbulence on your flight over here or something?

GRACE: Don't mind my sister, her English is still developing.

Beat.

DIVINE: Why don't I look for a couple extra Bibles upstairs and we can go over a little scripture before we end for today?

GRACE: Great idea.

BIEN-AIMÉ: I'll help you, Divine.

DIVINE and BIEN-AIMÉ exit.

GRACE: Why did you do that?

SARAH: Do what?

GRACE: Tu cherches toujours des problèmes là où il n'y en a pas. *(You always look for problems where there aren't any.)*

SARAH: Calme-toi. *(Calm down.)*

GRACE: Why are you bringing up all this nonsense about Pasteur Ben and Bien-Aimé? Like you know something—when you don't.

SARAH: Because Bien-Aimé is—whatever. Why are you defending her? She doesn't even like you anymore.

GRACE: What do you know?

SARAH: I know that the instant Bien-Aimé noticed Divine, you disappeared.

GRACE: Honestly, you talk too much.

SARAH: And you don't?

GRACE: You are jealous of Bien-Aimé. Because you couldn't get a boy's attention if your life depended on it. Too much fufu in your brain and not enough in your ass.

SARAH: Says you, pretending to know anything about *(She demonstrates vulgar and inaccurate blowjob gestures.)*

GRACE: Just because you are desperate to get on your knees for anything but prayer does not mean I am too.

SARAH: So are you pure or aren't you? Make up your mind.

GRACE: What happens between my sheets does not concern you.

SARAH: We share a room, sister, nothing happens between your sheets—except nightmares and period stains.

GRACE: Ta guele! *(Shut your mouth!)*

SARAH: Ta guele! *(You shut your mouth!)*

GRACE: Ozali zoba. *(You're an idiot.)*

SARAH: Yo pe nyama. *(You too, beast.)*

GRACE: Get your own brain. Or do I have to share that with you too?

SARAH: Shut up.

GRACE: No!

SARAH doesn't have a comeback.

They really should have left you in Bandundu, villageoise *(village girl).*

SARAH: Kinshasa.

GRACE: Hm. Right.

Lights dim on SARAH and GRACE as our focus goes to BIEN-AIMÉ and DIVINE upstairs.

BIEN-AIMÉ: Sorry about all that… Grace was better before Sarah arrived—don't tell them I said that, though.

DIVINE: No, of course not.

BIEN-AIMÉ: My mom was right about that family.

DIVINE: What do you mean?

BIEN-AIMÉ: Oh, just a little bit of drama they left behind in Congo—but I guess it followed them here. I shouldn't say, it's just songi songi.

DIVINE: What is songi songi?

BIEN-AIMÉ It's Lingala for rumours or like gossip.

DIVINE: There was a lot of that at Roxboro Faith, I'm not a fan. I prefer to give people grace. All rumours do is hurt.

BIEN-AIMÉ takes this in.

BIEN-AIMÉ: Wow. You're like really genuine, aren't you? Hm. *(Beat.)* So, where can we get an extra Bible for those two little demons? I'm kidding, I'm kidding. *(Looks up the heavens.)* Sorry, Jesus.

DIVINE: I have a spare key for the pastor's office, I'm pretty sure I saw some Bibles we can borrow in there.

BIEN-AIMÉ: Oh-la-la, a key to the pastor's office!

DIVINE: It's for emergencies, or to lock up any valuables. Since I'm technically a small group leader now…

BIEN-AIMÉ: What else do you have a key to?

DIVINE: I think Pasteur Ben gave me all the keys—and the codes to the building.

BIEN-AIMÉ: You must have made quite the impression on him.

DIVINE: I was—I am very passionate about this group.

BIEN-AIMÉ You're right. I'm sorry we haven't been taking it seriously. Talking about boys and sex, way too much.

DIVINE: It's okay. I'm just happy that you all showed up—despite my boring email invitation.

BIEN-AIMÉ: Yeah, fortunately for you my faith runs deep, so I'm still trying to give this church another chance.

DIVINE: Another chance?

BIEN-AIMÉ: Oh. Yeah, my dad is— was the senior pastor before Pasteur Ben—long story. But we still come to church… this is still our community. Where else would we go?

DIVINE: Well, I'm glad you joined my small group. And hopefully we can get more focused in the next sessions.

BIEN-AIMÉ: For sure. We should totally make up a plan for the next few sessions, you know, like an agenda that we can stick to.

DIVINE: …I already have one.

BIEN-AIMÉ: Of course you do.

DIVINE: It can be flexible, we're not at school, we can chillax—But those aren't the kinds of conversations I've ever had before… *(Whispers.)* about sex—

BIEN-AIMÉ: Divine, God can still hear you when you whisper. Your friends at school never talk about boys or hooking up?

DIVINE: Kind of. They talk about boys and—I don't know, maybe they don't get detailed in the conversation with me because I'm Christian.

BIEN-AIMÉ: Yeah, I don't think that's why.

DIVINE: What do you mean?

BIEN-AIMÉ: I'm Christian, doesn't stop my friends from having any kind of conversation with me. No offence, but it's because you're a prude. *(Beat.)* I said no offence!

DIVINE: Shoot… is it really that bad?

BIEN-AIMÉ: You just need to pull the stick a little bit out of your—Sorry. Okay, let's make a deal. I will continue to come to this small group every week with my radiant energy… and I'll make sure those other two show up as well, and we will fellowship and bond in Christ's blood and whatever. But you need to take some time to hang out with us, do normal teenage shit, okay? Nothing too crazy, but you need to loosen up a bit. A teeny bit, not full corruption… okay?

DIVINE: Nothing outrageous. I don't want to have to repent on an hourly basis. Promise?

BIEN-AIMÉ: I'll even swear on the Bible if you want.

DIVINE: I don't want that.

BIEN-AIMÉ: You're probably right. It still surprises me that God doesn't just strike me down once I set foot in here.

BIEN-AIMÉ laughs, DIVINE doesn't.

DIVINE: Do you want me to pray for you?

BIEN-AIMÉ: No, no, thank you. I—I was just kidding—Let's head back.

Scene Two

The girls are in the church basement. Their belongings are scattered all over the place. They are painting their nails and eating plantain chips.

SARAH: Can you help me paint my other hand?

GRACE: No.

SARAH: Grace… why not?

GRACE: Because I said no. No is no. Leave me alone.

SARAH: Fine. Sorry.

DIVINE: …Okay.

Silence. SARAH noisily eats chips.

SARAH: Okay…so can we talk about Pasteur Ben's new lady friend?

DIVINE: She's a new prospective member, I think.

BIEN-AIMÉ: Hmph, since when do new people get front row seats to Sunday service?

SARAH: Did you not see the way she was watching him preach? Her eyes looked like they might fall out of her head. I mean, he wasn't that inspiring.

BIEN-AIMÉ: Mhm, he was just repeating words Jesus said anyway, so…

SARAH: And a blouse that shows that much breast in a church is—

BIEN-AIMÉ: Ew. Why did you notice her breasts?

SARAH: I didn't—I—

BIEN-AIMÉ: Temptation is everywhere…You know, this is why the church can't have just one pastor. Men are feeble. All of our salvation is riding on the back of this one horny man.…

SARAH: Isn't that because your dad was fired?

BIEN-AIMÉ: Excuse me—

SARAH: Your dad was the senior pastor at church before, no? Tantine Rose Tshibangu said that—

BIEN-AIMÉ: I don't know what your random tantine said. But my father voluntarily stepped down from his duties, in order to focus on his family—il faut être Pasteur dans son propre foyer en premier. *(You have to be a pastor in your own home first.)*

GRACE: Yes. I wish my papa had taken some time off work as we all started to arrive in Canada… to make the transition easier.

BIEN-AIMÉ: Speaking of family, I heard your brother is arriving soon. Antoine? There was some trouble with his visa?

GRACE: Not trouble. You know how they are at the border. They see people arriving alone from a third world country and assume the worst. He must be seeking refugee status…

SARAH: He must have Ebola.

GRACE: He must be uneducated.

SARAH: He must be poor.

BIEN-AIMÉ: He must be a criminal.

DIVINE: Stereotyping is—

GRACE: Antoine has been stuck in Belgium for a few weeks now, but Papa confirmed they gave him the green light. He arrives tonight!

DIVINE: Do you miss it sometimes? Congo?

GRACE: No.

BIEN-AIMÉ: I was four when I left. So I'm like a tourist when I go back. La Canadienne. *(The Canadian.)*

SARAH: I miss it. The heat, the ease, the familiarity.

GRACE: So go back then.

Beat.

DIVINE: I can't believe no other girls showed up tonight…again. I thought my last email was better.

BIEN-AIMÉ: Don't take it personal, the girls at this church can be stuck up.

SARAH: I find them to be kind.

BIEN-AIMÉ: I'm sure you'd like more girls here.

SARAH: Divine does. And it's not her fault that no one else shows up.

DIVINE: Well, I am the group leader, I should be—

GRACE: What happened to your Holy Spirit of collaboration?

DIVINE: Oh—I didn't mean leader like—

GRACE: Why do you want more girls here? Are we not good enough for you?

DIVINE: No! I mean, yes! It's just that—at Roxboro there was—

GRACE: Argh, again with that mundele church.

DIVINE: Sorry. I—maybe on Sunday, after the service I can try talking to some of the other girls I've seen around? I just want everyone to feel welcome / to join us.

BIEN-AIMÉ: Forget those other girls. They saw the emails, if they wanted to join us, they'd be here, okay? So Divine, what colour do you want on your toes?

DIVINE: Beige. Like my hands.

BIEN-AIMÉ: You want that same, neutral, basic-ass colour on your toes, too?

DIVINE: It's not basic. Beige is easier to match. The rest are just a little too… loud… for me.

BIEN-AIMÉ: You have to pick something LOUD and vibrant for your toes. It's just for you… unless there is someone else seeing your toes that you're not telling us about.

SARAH: Oooooh.

GRACE: Oooooh.

DIVINE: What?! No—

SARAH: Look at her! If she was White she'd be all red right now.

GRACE: Who has seen your toes, mundele girl?

SARAH: Mhmm, if he's seen your toes, that means, he's seen your ankles…

GRACE: And probably your knees.

BIEN-AIMÉ: Who have you been exposing your knees to, Divine?

DIVINE: No one! Literally no one! *(Beat.)* No one even looks at me like that. And it's fine. Because I don't want to be looked at like that. Not necessarily anyway. But, no, no one has seen my toes. No one will see my toes.

SARAH: Are we still talking about toes?

GRACE: Shut up.

DIVINE: Let's do pink.

DIVINE picks out a bright pink bottle, hands it to BIEN-AIMÉ who starts to paint her toenails.

BIEN-AIMÉ: Everyone wants to be looked at like that. It's fun, to be desired. To show them what they can't have.

GRACE: Well, they can have a taste. If they've earned it.

SARAH: A nibble, as they say. Means a small bite.

DIVINE: Okay, but clearly I'm not like everyone else… Between the fact that I don't speak Lingala and my only friends are Jesus and his twelve disciples—it's like I'm from another planet.

GRACE: True.

BIEN-AIMÉ: You're not from another planet, Divine, you're just—

GRACE: Congolese on the outside, mundele at heart.

BIEN-AIMÉ: No! It's like…. it's like me. I have a million friends at school, but like what do any of them actually know about me? Especially the fact that I'm Congolese?

GRACE: Right, no one at our school knows anything about Congo.

BIEN-AIMÉ: And if they do, it's nothing good.

SARAH: Divine, you are a real Canadian. We still have our accents and our hair is…

GRACE: Don't even start with the hair thing. Why do mundele love to put their hands in here just like that? Without asking?! In Kinshasa, you would get a slap right across the face for that.

SARAH: Une bonne claque. *(A nice slap.)*

BIEN-AIMÉ: Literally, I've never worn my natural hair at school. But I'm thinking of doing a twist-out for convocation in June.

GRACE: With your big head, your graduation cap won't even fit.

SARAH: Do they really throw all those caps in the air, like in the American Hollywood movies?

BIEN-AIMÉ: Whatever, at least I still have my edges.

GRACE's hands cover her edges protectively.

GRACE: Hey, they're growing back!

DIVINE: I'm sure you're going to look amazing. Eric is a lucky guy.

BIEN-AIMÉ: You like talking about my man, don't you?

DIVINE: What?!

BIEN-AIMÉ: Relax, I'm joking. But yes, he is extremely lucky—

DIVINE: Oh my gosh! I can't believe I forgot to mention this before, but uh—speaking of Eric...apparently, he and some of the other guys at church asked Pasteur Ben about starting their own boys-only small group.

GRACE: Ha! To discuss what? Eating food and playing sports?

BIEN-AIMÉ: Oh, yeah! He mentioned that to me the other night. I forgot to tell you, girl.

DIVINE: It's kind of exciting... like maybe L'Église will start to have a lot more youth groups soon. Fellowship is so—

BIEN-AIMÉ: Important.

DIVINE: Yes, exactly!

BIEN-AIMÉ: Maybe... maybe, we should do a youth group night.

SARAH: Like a party?

GRACE: Oh, a party!

SARAH: My first Canadian party!

BIEN-AIMÉ: What? No. I never said a party. A youth group night. Basically, everyone at the church who isn't like twenty and old gets together for activities and worship.

DIVINE: Oh! At Roxboro Faith— *(GRACE gives DIVINE a look.)* Uh, my old church used to do that, like every couple of months!

BIEN-AIMÉ: Exactly! It gives us a chance to share what we're learning about God and whatever. Honestly, this church could use a bit of livening up. Things have changed, you know? It barely feels like a community anymore. Since Mama Jackie passed / God bless her soul, and the scandal with Ya Elize, it's been depressing every Sunday.

SARAH: God bless her soul. GRACE: God bless her soul.

DIVINE: I know I don't know—like how things used to be... but merging the youth groups at my old church was a lot of fun. It worked really well then... I know Pasteur Ben has some hesitations about—

BIEN-AIMÉ: But it's just one night.

DIVINE: Right... just one night...and if it goes well / then maybe—

BIEN-AIMÉ: Yeah, so maybe you can talk to Pasteur Ben about it? Feel it out, see what he thinks.

DIVINE: For sure, I can shoot him an email.

BIEN-AIMÉ: Oui, petite sœur. *(Yes, little sis.)* It's a wonderful opportunity for the church, so I'm sure he'll love your idea!

DIVINE: Your idea.

BIEN-AIMÉ: That's what I said, no?

GRACE: That's what I heard.

DIVINE: Oh, sorry.

GRACE: No worry, it happens to me all the time.

SARAH: That's because your English sucks.

GRACE: It's better than yours.

SARAH: You wish.

GRACE: You're the one who got put back into tenth grade even though you're soon to be eighteen.

SARAH: That's because I didn't go to the fancy international school like you.

GRACE: Hm. Clearly, you didn't inherit my papa's brains.

SARAH: C'est mon papa, aussi. *(He's my papa, too.)*

GRACE: Allegedly.

SARAH: I—

GRACE: What?

SARAH: Connasse. *(Stupid cow.)*

SARAH exits. Silence.

DIVINE: ...Maybe you should go after her?

GRACE: Ah, don't worry, Mundele. Just sister stuff...

DIVINE: I wouldn't know, I only have a little brother.

GRACE: Chanceuse. *(Lucky you.)*

DIVINE: I think you're lucky to have Sarah. I would have loved a sister, like a blood-related best friend.

GRACE: It's not always that simple.

BIEN-AIMÉ: My sister is way older and we still fought like cats and dogs.

GRACE: Eh eh, the cats and dogs fight here?

BIEN-AIMÉ: What?

DIVINE: It's an expression, because like cats and dogs really hate each other I guess. So people say fighting like cats and dogs.

GRACE: Hmm... but have you ever seen cats and dogs fight just like that, with your own two eyes?

BIEN-AIMÉ: That's not the point—

GRACE: They should say fighting like peacocks.

DIVINE: Why like peacocks?

GRACE: Only someone who has never seen peacocks fight would ask such a thing.

DIVINE: But—

GRACE: Trust me. Sisters fight like peacocks. Brothers like gorillas. I don't know who fights like cats and dogs, but that expression makes no sense. English is stupid.

DIVINE: Maybe it only feels like that because your English isn't good yet?

GRACE: Excuse me?!

DIVINE: No! Sorry, I—Sorry. I didn't mean it like that. I didn't mean to—uhm, should we… I'm really sorry. Should we get back to the Bible?

BIEN-AIMÉ: Ah yes, the Book of Ruth.

DIVINE: Yeah, I kinda expected us to move faster. This is our third meeting and we've only finished reading Chapter 1.

BIEN-AIMÉ: Do you want to read without Sarah?

DIVINE: Right… She still hasn't come back…

They look towards the exit.

DIVINE: Maybe—

BIEN-AIMÉ: Maybe we just call it an early night! We can read Chapter 2 next week.

GRACE: Good idea! If Sarah gets home way before me, Papa will have questions.

BIEN-AIMÉ and GRACE quickly begin to gather their things.

DIVINE: Okay, but let's pray before we head out.

GRACE lets out a groan. They bow their heads as DIVINE leads a short prayer. We hear DIVINE's prayer in the transition for the next scene.

"Father God, we are so blessed to be in your presence. Thank you for uniting us here in your house tonight. We cherish our oneness with you, and with each other. May your Holy Spirit continue to work within each of us individually as we learn to keep our hearts pure. We thank you for all we have learned today. May your wisdom continue to guide us as we go our separate ways. In Jesus's mighty name we pray, Amen."

Scene Three

DIVINE is alone in the church basement. She is daydreaming about her baptism. She stands at an imaginary podium, in front of the entire congregation of L'Église du Seigneur. All eyes on her. She takes centre stage and gives her testimony.

DIVINE: Dearly beloved, we are gathered here today for the rebirth of Divine Ntumba Kabamba. Never to be known again as "Mundele." Jeremiah 1:5 says "Before I formed you in the womb I knew you, before you were born I set you apart." God has always known who I am. And who I would become. And as I stand before you today, on the day of my baptism, I know that I am ready to become that woman he formed me to be. Today, I become One with the Father. And I am so grateful that I didn't rush into it because everyone else was doing it. I am so grateful for you all to witness my transformation. And it excites me / to completely surrender my life to God—

GRACE and SARAH rush in, startling DIVINE.

SARAH: Sorry we're late—eh eh, why are you on the table?

GRACE: And who are you talking to?

DIVINE: No one! I—I—

SARAH: You are always talking to yourself.

DIVINE: I'm not, I was praying—

GRACE: In Congo, people who talk to themselves too much are crazy.

SARAH: Are you crazy?

DIVINE: No! I— Why are you guys late again?

SARAH: Sorry!

GRACE: You should be, it is your fault we are late.

SARAH: Eh eh? You are the one who left your bus pass at home.

GRACE: Because you took my black purse again. Without asking. Again. And usually my bus pass is in the small pocket inside.

DIVINE pulls out her phone and sends a text to BIEN-AIMÉ (R u coming tonight??) She sees that BIEN-AIMÉ has read the message, no answer.

SARAH: You said I could borrow it.

GRACE: Liar! You are lying in the house of God. I hope He does not strike you down as we speak.

Beat.

He is merciful. You are lucky.

DIVINE: Have either of you heard from Bien-Aimé?

GRACE: No. Have not seen her since church on Sunday....

DIVINE: Oh, I was at her house yesterday but she said she would be—

GRACE: You were at Bien-Aimé's house?

DIVINE: Yeah.

SARAH: Bien-Aimé never invited you over.

GRACE: She did. Once or twice. Before you came to Canada. But I just had plans, so I didn't go.

SARAH: What plans?

GRACE: What do you care?

SARAH: I don't.

DIVINE: So, neither of you heard from her today?

SARAH: I would be surprised if she showed her face here.

DIVINE: Why?

SARAH and GRACE share a look.

GRACE: You saw Bien-Aimé yesterday?

DIVINE: Yes.

SARAH: And how did she seem?

DIVINE: She seemed fine. Normal? I—I don't know… why?

GRACE: Weren't you at church on Sunday?

DIVINE: No, my brother was sick so my parents—

SARAH: Mundele—

DIVINE: I've asked you not to call me that—

SARAH: Ah, it's a joke.

DIVINE: Whatever, I—

GRACE: She doesn't know.

SARAH: I cannot believe she doesn't know.

DIVINE: Know what?

GRACE: Her best friend didn't tell her.

SARAH: Had her all up in her house yesterday and didn't say a word.

GRACE: When everyone else knows.

SARAH: Everyone.

GRACE: What a friendship.

DIVINE: I don't—What are you…? Sorry! Sorry, but can you please just tell me what is going on.

GRACE: Eh eh, no need to be raising voices.

SARAH: Honestly…. my ears are sensitive.

DIVINE: Sorry, I—sorry.

GRACE: As I am a child of God, I forgive you.

SARAH: Bien-Aimé had a mental break!

DIVINE: What?

GRACE: I was going to say it! Why didn't you let me tell her?

SARAH: You were taking too long.

GRACE: You ruin everything.

DIVINE: What are you talking about?

SARAH: …Go ahead.

GRACE: Ekamuisi ngai! *(You would not believe!)* A mental breakdown. She went crazy in the church on Sunday.

SARAH: You missed quite the show.

DIVINE: Show—what… what happened?

GRACE: I don't know. All I know is after the Sunday service Eric Mwanza was talking to Joelle Wabantu, you know, close talking… and Bien-Aimé saw it and had a meltdown. She ran up to them, screaming and shouting and crying. In front of the whole church! Someone said she even threw a chair!

SARAH: I heard she was yelling at the Pastor! At Pasteur Ben! She was trying to get his attention, and it didn't work. So she started screaming and shouting and crying. Going on about her father being fired, and her family being banned from the church.

GRACE: After that spectacle they will be banned for sure.

SARAH: Eh, what church would take in a disgraced pastor and his screaming daughter.

GRACE: Screaming like a chimpanzee.

DIVINE: Stop. Stop! Did you see any of this? Either of you? With your own eyes?

GRACE: Just the same, we heard it.

SARAH: Everyone did.

DIVINE: With your own ears?

SARAH: Eh. With who else's ears would we hear?

DIVINE: I mean—is this just more songi songi? *(gossip, rumours?)*

GRACE: Oh! Yes.

SARAH: But it's true, Mundele. Everyone at church was talking about it. If everyone is saying it, it has to be true. I bet you could even ask Eric himself.

GRACE: Or Pasteur Ben! He always tells the truth, he is a man of God.

SARAH: Yeah, everyone knows Christians don't lie. It's a sin.

DIVINE: Why wouldn't Bien-Aimé tell me any of this? I saw her yesterday. We were / hanging out—

GRACE: Then where is she?

SARAH: Hiding!

DIVINE: She's not hiding! She has nothing to hide from!

GRACE: Do you see her here?

SARAH: It's not her fault. She is ashamed.

GRACE: I don't blame her.

DIVINE: No, she's not—I was with her yesterday. She was fine!

GRACE: Mhmm, you were with her all day and she didn't tell you…

SARAH: Shame!

GRACE: Mundel—Divine. We are only telling you this, because we care about you. Bien-Aimé sometimes, can be, a bit of, a—

SARAH: Liar.

GRACE: Yes, so we want you to—

DIVINE: No. Bien-Aimé has been nothing but nice to me. And sincere. If there was anything to tell me, she would have, so… I don't—I don't want to hear any more nonsense like this, okay? I don't know why you— why you're always— but I don't want to hear it anymore.

DIVINE pulls out her Bible, it lands on the table with a loud thump.

DIVINE: So, are we reading this or what?

Scene Four

BIEN-AIMÉ struts into the church basement humming a hymn. She is caught off guard by SARAH sitting alone at the table, reading a book.

BIEN-AIMÉ: Oh! Qu'est-ce que tu fais ici en silence comme ça? *(What are you doing here silently like that?)*

SARAH holds up her book to indicate what she's doing and keeps reading.

Where's Grace?

SARAH shrugs.

You know, Sarah, as the pastor's daughter I consider it my duty to check in on our congregation. How are you adjusting to your new life in Canada?

SARAH: It is good. Thank you, Bien-Aimé, I am so blessed to have a sister in Christ who cares as much as you do.

SARAH turns back to her book. BIEN-AIMÉ recalibrates.

BIEN-AIMÉ: Are you good at keeping secrets, Sarah?

SARAH: What are you talking about?

BIEN-AIMÉ: I was just wondering if it runs in the family—since your father is so bad at keeping secrets. Because if he were any good, you'd still be in Congo, wouldn't you? Daddy's little secret side baby.

SARAH: I was never a secret. Papa was—it's just… private.

BIEN-AIMÉ Hmph, did you inherit that naiveté from your mistress mother? What was the fantasy she told you? That one day your part-time daddy would walk away from his real family in Kinshasa to come shack up in the bush in Bandundu? Please.

SARAH: It wasn't like that—

BIEN-AIMÉ: Plenty of men back home bring their extra children to live with their main family, they have no shame… so why did he leave you apart for so long?

SARAH is silenced.

Yeah. Must be naiveté. That's what's got you flapping those big lips to say anything about me, my dad or that stupid Pasteur Ben. Tu comprends? *(You understand me?)* You just got here and you don't know shit about me or my church, petite soeur. *(little sis.)* But I'm still trying to be a good Christian, so don't push me.

SARAH: You don't—You don't know a thing about us.

BIEN-AIMÉ: Oh, I don't? Grace's mom might seem like a quiet woman, but she was very open with my mom about all her feelings about you.

SARAH is silenced.

That poor woman has to see your face in her house every day and be reminded of her husband's mistake. And poor Grace / who—

SARAH: You don't scare me, Bien-Aimé. I see you for who you are. You use people to get what you want and then just throw them away. Comme tu l'as fait avec Grace! *(Like you did to Grace!)* You act like you are nice, but you just want to hurt people, that's why you have no friends left here.

BIEN-AIMÉ: I'm not the one here who hurt Grace.

SARAH: I have never hurt Grace. She is my sister.

BIEN-AIMÉ: Then why are you here?

SARAH: What?

BIEN-AIMÉ: Why did you come to Canada and ruin her life?

SARAH: I didn't— My Papa brought me here. He wanted me to be with my family.

BIEN-AIMÉ scoffs.

BIEN-AIMÉ: Is that what he told you? Ohhhh, the way men lie.

SARAH: You have a wicked heart. You want to bring trouble on my family like you did your own.

BIEN-AIMÉ: My family is perfect. You don't know what you're talking about.

SARAH: "First, take the plank out of your own eye / before you—"

BIEN-AIMÉ: Don't quote scripture / at me.

SARAH: Are you mad because it's true? Look what you did to your family. Your father should be preaching on Sundays not sitting / down in shame like—

BIEN-AIMÉ: And your father should actually love you and not have to be blackmailed / by a village woman—

SARAH: He does love me and—

BIEN-AIMÉ: Does he? Because Grace's mom says otherwise. You know he wanted to do DNA test on you? But that Katende family nose is hard to deny.

SARAH: No… my papa loves me. He always came to see me—every birthday he was there. He knows I'm his real daughter. My family has nothing to hide.

BIEN-AIMÉ: But you're hiding something, aren't you? Grace's mom said she has never seen a girl who refuses to wear dresses and skirts. A girl who would rather play / outside with the boys—

SARAH: I don't know what you're talking about.

BIEN-AIMÉ: Mmm, I think you do.

SARAH: It's not true.

BIEN-AIMÉ: You shouldn't lie in God's house.

BIEN-AIMÉ dissects SARAH with her gaze. SARAH squirms.

SARAH: You are a bitch.

BIEN-AIMÉ: Only when pushed— *(She sees DIVINE entering and shifts into a kinder voice.)* But, we are quickly approaching some big events for the church in the next few weeks. Youth group night and spring baptisms. So if you have any ideas, don't hesitate to share them!

DIVINE: MBOTE! Sango Nini! *(HELLO! Greetings!)*

BIEN-AIMÉ: That… that is… progress!

DIVINE: I wanna practise my Lingala in my baptism speech. I actually just finished it; I'm really excited about it!

DIVINE greets SARAH with the traditional three kisses and gives BIEN-AIMÉ a huge hug.

BIEN-AIMÉ: Praise God, let's just hope you don't have people falling asleep in their seats.

DIVINE: I won't!

BIEN-AIMÉ: I guess we'll see, eh, Sarah?

SARAH: So much to be seen.

BIEN-AIMÉ: So what's on the agenda for tonight?

DIVINE: I want to finally finish up the Book of Ruth and do a short study on her marriage to Boaz. And then, for the activity I was thinking we could make vision boards / I brought some magazines and —

GRACE: I HAVE ARRIVED!

GRACE bursts into the space like a tornado. She thumps down the stairs inelegantly carrying a huge basin filled with liquid.

BIEN-AIMÉ: What are you—

GRACE: My sisters!

SARAH: T'es malade toi? *(Are you crazy or what?)*

GRACE: Nope. Just filled with the Holy Spirit. *(She celebrates.)* I am sorry I am late, but I came with gifts. Also the Lord says to forgive seven hundred seventy seventy-seven seven… seven… times—I don't know, whatever, just forgive. I am here now.

DIVINE: What's in the bowl?

GRACE: I am so glad you asked, Mundele! It's an old Katende family recipe. Right, Sarah?

SARAH: Uhm—

DIVINE: Recipe for what?

GRACE: I brought cups!

GRACE pulls out cups from her backpack, dips them into the basin and fills them with the liquid inside. She passes one to each of the girls. DIVINE sniffs it curiously, it smells sweet, and she is intrigued, but something about GRACE's behaviour has her on edge.

GRACE: Who's going to pray over it? *(Beat.)* Sarah, vas-y. *(Go ahead.)*

SARAH: Uh—okay… uhh Jesus— God. Jesus. Sir. —Can you uh…

GRACE: Eh eh, c'est quoi ton problème? *(What's your problem?)*

DIVINE: Why do we need to pray before we drink it?

BIEN-AIMÉ: Oh, wow, aren't you the one who said that "to have food and drink is a merciful blessing"?

SARAH: And that "every meal and every drink is a miracle" ?

DIVINE: Okay, yes. But I am trying to—

GRACE: Ah ah ah!

BIEN-AIMÉ: I'll pray. Jesus, bless this drink we will share together tonight. Where faith is weak, dear Lord, reveal that all you give is good. Amen?

SARAH: Amen.

GRACE: Amen.

DIVINE: … Amen

GRACE and BIEN-AIMÉ toast and take large sips. SARAH takes a small sip. DIVINE hesitates.

DIVINE: Seriously, what is it?

GRACE: It is a family recipe, I told you. If you had ever bothered to come to Congo, you would know… It is just juice. Le Jus de la Verité. *(Truth Juice.)*

DIVINE: Truth Juice… so is there alcohol in it?

BIEN-AIMÉ: T'inquiète, Divine. *(Don't worry, Divine.)* I won't let you drink too much. We'll just have a bit of fun, eh? The Book of Ruth and a glass of Truth.

BIEN-AIMÉ throws up her cup for another toast, SARAH and GRACE say "Cheers" with her. They wait for DIVINE who reluctantly joins in. DIVINE takes a small sip.

DIVINE: It's actually not bad.

SARAH: It's juice. You'll be okay.

DIVINE: Why do you call it truth juice though?

GRACE: Watch. Ask me anything.

DIVINE: I don't know.

GRACE: Truly and really, ask me anything you want to know about me. And watch the truth just splash all over.

DIVINE: Okay… what's your favourite colour?

SARAH: Is she serious?

BIEN-AIMÉ: Whoa, okay. No. Ask her something better than that, please.

DIVINE: I don't know, what is there to ask?

GRACE: I don't know, ask me what's the last lie I told? Or who I would kill if I could get away with murder? Something fun, come on!

DIVINE: I feel like we have different definitions of fun.

DIVINE takes another sip. She likes the taste of the juice. Slowly, she begins to relax. She continues to take sporadic sips over the course of the scene. SARAH chugs her cup and immediately goes for a refill.

Whoa.

SARAH: Okay okay okay, I have a question.

GRACE: Ugh, fine. It better be good.

SARAH: Shut up and let me ask. Okay. Who would you rather French kiss: Eric Mwanza, Pasteur Ben, or Papa Thomas who cleans the church?

BIEN-AIMÉ: Why on earth would you choose—

SARAH: My question, my rules.

GRACE: I…

SARAH: Truth juice. You have to tell the truth, or God will turn you into a pillar of salt. Go.

DIVINE: Well, I don't think God would—

SARAH: Shh. Go!

GRACE covers her eyes with her hands.

GRACE: Eric Mwanza. *(She peeks out slowly from behind her hands.)* I'm sorry, Bien-Aimé, truth juice. I would never mess with your man but—I would never kiss those old men.

DIVINE: Pasteur Ben isn't that old…

SARAH: Oh, so you are under his spell too! That's why you are always sending SMS and emails.

DIVINE: No no no. I mean—I think we'd all pick Eric Mwanza, hands down. He's hot. *(Beat.)* This really is truth juice.

BIEN-AIMÉ chugs her remaining cup. Stands up and heads to serve herself more.

BIEN-AIMÉ: Eric, hmph.

DIVINE: What about him?

BIEN-AIMÉ: Well, he's up for grabs for any of you ladies because he's single.

GRACE: Eh eh, single?

BIEN-AIMÉ: He—we're… on a break.

DIVINE: Truth juice?

BIEN-AIMÉ: Truth juice. A very, extended, mostly permanent break. Happened last night.

SARAH: So you broke up?

GRACE: What happened?

DIVINE: Are you okay?

SARAH: Did he leave you?

BIEN-AIMÉ: It turns out he's not the guy I thought he was. I excepted him to be patient with me but, I… I… I don't know. I guess I wasn't worth the wait.

DIVINE: Do you mean… sex?

BIEN-AIMÉ: Yes, I mean sex… Guys have this stupid idea that sex makes a relationship stronger, like we'll have a bond we didn't have before. And I'm like, if I've already put all of you in my mouth, why isn't that bond strong enough? I just wanted to wait… I tried to explain it to him, but it was the same thing every time we hung out, always pawing at me. Begging, pleading, "Viens ici Bien-Aimé, s'il te plait Bien-Aimé" *("Come here Bien-Aimé, Please Bien-Aimé")* — It was just a lot. And it's not like I didn't want to. Hello?

DIVINE: Do you think it's love?

BIEN-AIMÉ: I thought so… maybe.

DIVINE: Wow.

BIEN-AIMÉ: I guess all guys just want one thing…

SARAH: But, you have had sex before, no?

BIEN-AIMÉ: No?

SARAH: I thought that's what Grace had told me.

GRACE: No! I—I would not—

BIEN-AIMÉ: Truth juice, confuse juice, eh? *(To GRACE.)* Don't worry about it.

DIVINE: I'm sorry about you and Eric though, Bien-Aimé. I thought—

SARAH: Okay, someone ask me a question.

BIEN-AIMÉ and GRACE are quiet as DIVINE takes a big swig of her drink.

DIVINE: Me! *(She raises her hand.)* What's up with you two? Sometimes you are like—*(DIVINE struggles to use hand gestures to clarify what she means.)* and then it's like—it's just—I… I don't get it.

GRACE: Huh?

DIVINE: Between you two!

SARAH: Who?

DIVINE: You and your sister, duh!

GRACE: What about us?

DIVINE: I know I don't have a sister but still—

BIEN-AIMÉ: It's a bit toxic.

SARAH: No—

BIEN-AIMÉ: Or maybe it's jealousy.

SARAH: No—

BIEN-AIMÉ: Or—

DIVINE: Ah ah ah! Truth juice. Tell the truth, Sarah.

SARAH: You haven't even asked a question.

GRACE: I forgot to say before! Rules. Rule 1 of the game, tell the truth. Number 2, cone of truth.

GRACE mimics putting a cone on her head.

BIEN-AIMÉ: She means cone of silence.

GRACE: Yes!

DIVINE: Scout's honour.

GRACE: Who is Scout?

BIEN-AIMÉ: Oh my go—Yes, yes, no one will say anything. Now, answer the question, Sarah.

SARAH: What is the question?!

BIEN-AIMÉ: Okay, why do you hate your sister?

DIVINE: No! No no, that's not my question. My question is…hold on…You're both seventeen, but you're in different grades, but you're sisters—wait, are you twins?

SARAH: No. Next question.

DIVINE: Wait, what?!

GRACE: You asked, she answered. Next!

DIVINE: But—

BIEN-AIMÉ: Don't worry, Divine, I'll explain it to you later.

GRACE: I want to ask you, Bien-Aimé.

BIEN-AIMÉ: Honestly, no. I just answered a question before about Eric.

GRACE: No one asked you. You just volunteered your drama.

BIEN-AIMÉ: My drama?

DIVINE: She means your story. You know her English is…uh… in a development stage.

SARAH: Ha! I told you.

GRACE: It is just a game, Bien-Aimé, let me ask you a question.

BIEN-AIMÉ: Can you get off my back, Grace? I just broke up with the love of my life. I'm a wreck.

DIVINE: Ask me a question!

SARAH whispers in GRACE's ear. GRACE giggles.

GRACE: D'accord, Divine. *(Okay, Divine.)* Who was your first kiss?

DIVINE: ...What?

SARAH: Did she not hear?

GRACE: Eh eh, open your ears!

BIEN-AIMÉ: Answer the question, Divine, you know the rules!

DIVINE: I know, I just—I haven't had my first kiss.

SARAH: MENTEUSE. *(LIAR.)* C'est une menteuse. *(She's a liar.)*

GRACE: You can't lie! Truth juice! Truth juice!

DIVINE: I'm not lying! Why would I lie?

BIEN-AIMÉ: Are you serious?

DIVINE: Yes, lying is a sin. And honestly, if I was going to lie, I would just make up some imaginary boy and say I kissed him.

SARAH: Whoa....

GRACE: Like no one? You have never put your lips on another human?

DIVINE: Well, yeah—like not in that… way—like family kisses on the cheek or whatever, but never my lips on another human boy's lips.

SARAH: …or girl?

DIVINE: Or girl…

GRACE: Eh, Mundele… what have you been doing with your life?

DIVINE: What do you mean?

GRACE: Before us, what was your fun?

DIVINE: Well, now that you mention it, I actually taught myself to play the clarinet last summer and it's been—

BIEN-AIMÉ: Okay, okay, leave her alone. *(To DIVINE.)* You're holding out for your special someone. Kinda like me. You deserve that.

SARAH: I have kissed at least six boys and one— But since I've arrived in Canada, nothing. So maybe I'll start over, back to zéro for North America, you know?

GRACE: Yeah, me too! Back to zéro in Canada. Clean plate!

SARAH: Let's play a game, let's see who can get a first kiss at the party next weekend.

GRACE: Yes!

BIEN-AIMÉ: Why not.

DIVINE: I don't know…

BIEN-AIMÉ: You don't have to if you don't want to.

GRACE: Yes, she does! Mundele is always the boring blanket. Have some fun with us for once.

DIVINE: I participate! There's just certain—

SARAH: Come on! For you, we can allow a cheek or forehead kiss, okay? Doesn't have to be on the lips.

BIEN-AIMÉ: Might be fun… it will give you some practice for the real thing one day…

DIVINE: Okay, maybe, I'll do a cheek or forehead / kiss…

GRACE: Eek!

DIVINE: Maybe!

SARAH: First one to get a kiss during the party next week wins… they just win! I don't know. A kiss is a win, no?

BIEN-AIMÉ: That's a bit juvenile, but whatever.

GRACE: BUT, it can't be someone you've kissed before. Bien-Aimé, that means Eric is off-limits to you.

SARAH: And surely a few others…

BIEN-AIMÉ: Oh, shut up already. Anyway, how do we prove who got a kiss? A picture?

DIVINE: No, that's—we're all Christians, right? Can't we all just promise to be honest? Truth juice.

They all nod in agreement.

I'm getting sweaty just thinking about it.

GRACE: It's exciting, Mundele. You'll get to give your Yaya *(your big sister)* Bien-Aimé a run for her money with these boys.

BIEN-AIMÉ: Oh, please.

GRACE: What? You think you're the only one the boys look at?

SARAH: You think no one notices the rest of us or what?

BIEN-AIMÉ: I didn't say that.

GRACE: You're just so used to being mwasi kitoko *(the pretty pretty girl)* all the time that you just forget that some people actually think we are sexy too.

SARAH: Yeah! I'm sexy!

DIVINE: Sexy is a bit… I don't… no one is calling me sexy.

SARAH: Wake up, Mundele. You have a fat butt. That means sexy, even if your personality is so-so.

BIEN-AIMÉ: We get it, Sarah, you like Divine's butt.

SARAH: What? No, I—

BIEN-AIMÉ: I think it's time to cut off the truth juice, hmm? Have some water instead?

BIEN-AIMÉ grabs the cups from the girls and exits to find water.

DIVINE: Yeah, I definitely need water.

SARAH: On the for real, Tantine Rose Tshibangu was right about Bien-Aimé.

GRACE: Mhm, that girl is the Queen of songi songi all the time.

DIVINE: She's not. I know that maybe you kinda knew Bien-Aimé before, but I think now maybe you don't know her as well as I do. She gets me. We get each other… Bien-Aimé is pretty much my best friend now, so…

GRACE: So, she tells you everything?

DIVINE: Yeah, we tell each other—

GRACE: But you didn't know about her mental breakdown at church last week?

DIVINE: It wasn't a mental break—

GRACE: And she didn't tell you about her and Eric?

DIVINE: It just happened.

SARAH: Mmm, allegedly.

DIVINE: What do you mean?

GRACE: When is the last time you saw them together?

SARAH: Or ever!

DIVINE: Uhm... at church, a few Sundays ago... I think? I'm sure I've seen them together.

SARAH: But not together-together, right?

GRACE: Holding hands? Hugging? Kissing?

SARAH: Touching butts?

DIVINE: No! I mean not—

GRACE: You see!

DIVINE: Maybe they're just private!

GRACE: Private, sure. But a secret? No. A secret is something to hide...

SARAH: Like humiliation.

GRACE: Or lies.

SARAH: Or—

DIVINE: No! Like who would do PDA in a church? This is literally a holy place— I'm sure they do… whatever it is they do… at school, or when they're alone— A few days ago when Bien-Aimé was at my house she left early to go meet up with Eric so. Plus, you know how her parents are—how all our parents are! And, her dad is a pastor, she can't just be seen frolicking with boys all over the place.

SARAH: Was a pastor. Not anymore.

DIVINE: Look, I don't know what you two are getting at, but you know I don't like to gossip. So let's just stop this. Now.

DIVINE begins to clean up.

SARAH: Eh eh, sorry, Mundele.

Silence.

GRACE: I just find it strange that I have NEVER seen them together—as a couple, the way she paints the picture to be.

SARAH: Me neither.

GRACE: Truth juice… I think Eric left Bien-Aimé months ago.

SARAH: If they were ever even really together!

GRACE: I think it happened before Christmas actually.

SARAH: Why?

GRACE: Because she told me that Eric bought her a promise ring for Christmas. BUT… I was talking to Joelle Wabantu and she told me her little sister works at the jewellery store in the mall. And she said that two weeks before

Christmas, Bien-Aimé went into her store and bought herself that exact ring!

SARAH: Eh! Wow!

DIVINE: What? That doesn't prove anything. And how does Joelle Wabantu's little sister even remember that?

GRACE: Please! You think she would forget something as pathetic as a girl buying herself a ring right before Christmas?

SARAH: I wouldn't. And everyone from L'Église would recognize Bien-Aimé.

GRACE: I think Eric Mwanza left Bien-Aimé like everyone else did, when her father was chased out of his position at the church.

SARAH: Out of embarrassment?

GRACE: For sure! She went from here *(GRACE gestures high up.)* to here *(She gestures down low.)* very quick.

DIVINE: What do you mean?

GRACE: There is no higher position in the church than the pastor, and then his family.

SARAH: Do you really think Bien-Aimé has been lying to us—to everyone—about her and Eric for this long?

GRACE: Yes.

SARAH: It's like Tantine said, she's the troubled daughter of the Pastor. Ex-pastor, actually.

DIVINE: ...Do you know why her dad stepped down?

SARAH: We shouldn't say. It's not proper to repeat people's business like that.

GRACE: We only overheard Tantine telling Papa the story. So we don't know 100%.

SARAH: But we can probably find out for you. Tantine always has lots to say about Bien-Aimé.

GRACE: Everyone does…

DIVINE: No! No, never mind I—I don't need to know or anything. I was just—I trust Bien-Aimé and if she wants me to know, she'll say so.

SARAH: Or lie about it. But whatever.

DIVINE: We really should have finished the Book of Ruth tonight… next week, can the four of us meet here a bit early before the party, uh—youth group night—and finish up our study?

GRACE: Yes! We can try out party outfits for each other.

BIEN-AIMÉ returns with the cups filled with water for each of them. DIVINE chugs hers quickly.

BIEN-AIMÉ: It's not a party, it's a youth group night. Same thing we always do, worship, prayer / Bible study, some activities—

SARAH: Pfffft, this party was your idea anyway. Probably an excuse to get alone time with Eric. Not that you need it anymore—

DIVINE: OKAY. One: everyone needs to stop calling it a party, it's youth group night. Two: Get here early on Friday and bring your Bibles. Three: Let's pray and go home, my head is starting to hurt.

They bow their heads as DIVINE begins to pray.

Scene Five

In the church basement, the night of the Youth Group "Party." Their clothes, make-up and other belongings are scattered all around. On their table is a fresh basin of homemade Truth Juice. There is also a bottle of tequila and some pre-sliced lemons in a plastic bag. The girls are in a circle holding hands, eyes closed, their heads bowed in prayer.

BIEN-AIMÉ: … and God, please look out for Divine tonight as she finally learns to mingle with the opposite sex. May she feel the presence of the Holy Spirit as she searches for lips to finally—

DIVINE: Okay, that's enough!

BIEN-AIMÉ: In the name of Jesus Christ, we pray…

The girls say "AMEN" in unison.

But seriously, maybe you'll find the Boaz to your Ruth tonight.

SARAH: The Joseph to your Mary.

GRACE: Ugh, not Joseph and Mary. She was a virgin, that's what we're trying to avoid with this one.

DIVINE: Can we please talk about something else?

SARAH: Mundele, are you nervous?

DIVINE: I… I don't know. I've never even gone to a school dance. I don't know what I'm doing.

GRACE: Do boys make you nervous?

BIEN-AIMÉ: Those aren't nerves, Divine…

DIVINE: What?

BIEN-AIMÉ: That tingle you feel… from deep inside you… it's sexual desire.

DIVINE: We're in a church! Don't … don't say things like that.

BIEN-AIMÉ: It's a Friday night, God's not here right now. He has better things to do.

DIVINE: Maybe I shouldn't be here for this. I really thought it was going to be a night of worship and fellowship. I didn't expect all this—

GRACE receives a text message.

GRACE: EEEK! Our brother Antoine is coming tonight… with his friend David Lavoie-Bilolo.

SARAH: No way!

GRACE: Rifle! Rifle!

BIEN-AIMÉ: What?!

GRACE: Rifle! He is mine, no one else can touch because I said rifle first.

SARAH: Oh my—

GRACE: Don't hate.

DIVINE: No, it's "shotgun," not rifle. You can't go around screaming "rifle," people will call the police.

GRACE: Rifle, shotgun, machete, whatever—he's mine. Hands off.

DIVINE: Who is this David Lavoie anyway?

SARAH: Out of reach for you, Mundele, even with that fat fufu butt of yours.

BIEN-AIMÉ: He's not even all that. He's just exotic to you people because his mother is Quebecois and his dad is Congolese.

DIVINE: So he's biracial?

BIEN-AIMÉ: Yeah, that's it. But when he used to come to the church—every tantine was like "Oh il est beau, oh il est clair, oh il est grand" *("Oh he's good looking, oh he's so light, oh he's so tall")* — the guy barely finished high school. He only got into university because of his basketball talents.

GRACE: That's how Antoine knows him, they both go to the university—

BIEN-AIMÉ: Aren't they too old for this party anyway? Don't they have girls their own age they can be spending a Friday night with?

SARAH: Antoine isn't even twenty yet.

BIEN-AIMÉ: Hmm, so you say. Everyone knows his papers were forged to get him into Canada.

GRACE: Why would you say that?

BIEN-AIMÉ: Canada doesn't open its border to immigrants with criminal records, so... *(A long beat.)* I'm just teasing. It's a joke.

GRACE: I told you that in confidence. My brother didn't steal anything. The shop owner—

BIEN-AIMÉ: Let's drop it. I don't care how old your brother is or isn't.

SARAH: Because you just prefer your men over the age of thirty, right?

BIEN-AIMÉ: Pardon? *(Excuse me?)*

DIVINE: Uhm, I thought we were dropping it.

SARAH: So you just prefer to be involved with men over the age of thirty?

GRACE: Sarah, c'est assez. *(Sarah, that's enough.)*

BIEN-AIMÉ: I'm pretty tired of your little side comments.

SARAH: And I'm sick of yours. You always have something to say about my family.

BIEN-AIMÉ: I just say what I know, you just talk out of your fat ass.

SARAH: Except I know things too, Bien-Aimé, we all know how you destroyed your family.

DIVINE: Whoa, I don't / think we need to lose our cool—

GRACE pulls DIVINE back.

BIEN-AIMÉ: Maybe you should tell your "sister" the real reason you came to Canada.

GRACE: What are you saying?

SARAH: She's a liar.

BIEN-AIMÉ: Am I?

SARAH: That's what Pasteur Ben says.

BIEN-AIMÉ slaps SARAH, her eyes filled with rage and tears.

BIEN-AIMÉ: Shut the fuck up.

SARAH is in shock. She presses her hand to her cheek. No one dares breathe. BIEN-AIMÉ goes to pick up her bag, pulls out a bottle of red wine and exits the room. DIVINE stands still for a moment, unsure of what to do.

GRACE: Go.

DIVINE snaps out of it and rushes after BIEN-AIMÉ upstairs. GRACE rushes to the table, puts her bare hand into the basin of Truth Juice pulls an ice cube out. She rushes back to SARAH to lay it against her face. Our focus is with DIVINE and BIEN-AIMÉ. BIEN-AIMÉ is pacing and sipping red wine directly from the bottle.

DIVINE: Are you okay?

BIEN-AIMÉ: Only you would watch me beat up another girl and ask if I'm okay.

DIVINE: I think beat up is a bit strong…

BIEN-AIMÉ: I can't believe I just did that.

DIVINE: I'm not really sure what just happened.

BIEN-AIMÉ: I thought I was more in control…

DIVINE: Sarah was being really—I'm sorry, I should have—you're not a liar.

BIEN-AIMÉ: No one is perfect.

DIVINE: No, obviously not. But calling you a liar and saying that—

BIEN-AIMÉ: And if I am?

DIVINE: What?

BIEN-AIMÉ: What if I told you Sarah is right that I'm a liar—

DIVINE: I don't—

BIEN-AIMÉ: Don't you see it? I'm a leper, Divine.

DIVINE: No, you're not. Why would you say that?

BIEN-AIMÉ: Have you ever seen a pastor's daughter at church that people avoid as much as me? / They all just—

DIVINE: Is this about what happened after Sunday service a few weeks ago? Grace and Sarah said something about a breakdown—

BIEN-AIMÉ: Is that what they're calling it? *(Beat.)* Eric and I got into a stupid fight— disagreement—after that service. He has a picture of me that… I just want to make sure he deleted it like he promised. We haven't talked since our breakup—he won't talk to me. He acts like I don't even / exist. So, yeah, I got upset—

DIVINE: Wait…hold on, I thought you broke up after that "mental breakdown" or whatever…

BIEN-AIMÉ: What?

DIVINE: You and Eric got in the fight or disagreement or whatever at church and then the week after you told us you broke up…

BIEN-AIMÉ: Right. Yeah, yeah…. I…. Fuck… Divine, I'm sorry, I— *(Beat.)* Eric and I, we broke up way before. Before you and I even met…. I just kept lying because—

DIVINE: Because what? Bien-Aimé, why would you lie to me for so long about something like that? That's so—I—I don't get it.

BIEN-AIMÉ: I know. I'm so sorry. I—I don't even know where to start—I…I'll explain, okay? If you can just listen and— Everyone I've told they… they don't get it. And you, you always have my back. I don't want that to change.

DIVINE: Because you're my best friend and I—I want to have your back, Bien-Aimé, but not if you're lying to me about stuff like that—big, life stuff like that—

BIEN-AIMÉ: I know. I know— I wanted to tell you before. I just didn't know… Okay…

A long beat.

A lot happened before you came to L'Église… Before Mama Jackie died last August, she was sick for a while—like in and out of the hospital for like two years. And Pasteur Ben got pretty close to our family, he was alone a lot and… and my dad kinda took him under his wing… he would be at our house, for dinners, or meetings with my dad and whatever. Last June, I got my learner's licence, and Pasteur Ben was super nice, he would always offer to take me driving for a bit. He said he liked the distraction. I got to practise parallel parking, and he'd get to think about something other than his wife dying. We'd drive around my neighbourhood a few times a week, like twenty, thirty minutes, an hour, whatever… And we would just talk, about everything and nothing. He was cool. And my parents didn't mind because then they didn't have to take me driving. And they trusted him. Because of the church. He was like family. I trusted him… This one day he was really upset. Mama Jackie hadn't been doing well and he came by and had dinner with me and my parents, and then I asked if he wanted to go driving. He kinda didn't want to, but I… I insisted. I pushed. So we went. He was giving me directions, and we were driving for a long time, and we ended up kinda far away, at this construction site by the water. It was dead quiet. I parked the car. I was gonna text my mom, but he grabbed my phone. I freaked out. He started apologizing and then he started crying. It was weird. I didn't know what to do. What do you do when a grown man is suddenly sobbing in front of you? So I gave him a hug. I thought it'd be awkward, but it was kinda nice. I made him feel better. I felt good. But then the hug lasted like, too long? I tried to pull away, but he held me tighter. His hands slid further and further. Down my back. Around front to my… my breasts. I kinda froze. I didn't know what to do or say. His breath was hot against my face. His lips pressed against my ear, whispering my name over and over. He said it so much, I started to hate my name. "Viens ici, Bien-Aimé, s'il te plait, Bien Aimé…. J'ai besoin de ça." *("Come here, Bien-Aimé, Please, Bien-Aimé, I need this.")* I tried to say something. He covered my mouth with his. Silencing me. Forcing his tongue in my mouth. And I… I just closed my eyes and tried not to cry until—until he was finished. I don't even remember how I ended up in the passenger seat, but he drove home. Before I got out of the car, he said we needed to pray. Repent. So we did. He asked God to forgive me for tempting him. And to forgive him for falling into my temptation. Before I left, he told me that I couldn't tell anyone if I wanted true repentance. "Your silence will be your salvation," he said, like he was quoting scripture. I believed it. I got out of the car, went into my house and went to bed, like nothing happened. It was between me, him and God. I wasn't gonna tell— But then it kept happening. All summer. He kept taking me for drives and… every time I kept thinking, this is the one, this is gonna be the last time, and I—I just wanted it to go back to normal, before he— And every time, praying for forgiveness, asking God to make us stop, like I was choosing to— I—I just wanted it to stop. I needed it to stop. And then it did. Because Mama Jackie got worse and worse and he wasn't coming over anymore, and I could breathe again. And then that weekend before school started, she died. And he came for dinner, and he was crying. But this time, I didn't feel bad. I felt angry. Seeing him hugging my dad and— Something in me snapped. I couldn't do it. I refused to come to dinner. Lied to my mom, said I was sick and staying in bed. She knew something was up and I knew I'd have tell her the truth or keep lying. So, I told her the truth.

DIVINE has been holding her breath. She finally releases it.

DIVINE: I don't know what to say…I—Shit… Bien-Aimé, I—I'm so sorry. That's—horrible. Horrible doesn't even seem like the right word. But I'm really sorry you went through that.

BIEN-AIMÉ: Don't be sorry. It's—honestly, that wasn't the worst part for me.

DIVINE: What do you mean?

BIEN-AIMÉ takes a sip of wine and hands it to DIVINE who takes a large gulp as well.

BIEN-AIMÉ: My mom. She believed me at first, when I told her that night. She held me. Cried with me. "Pas mon bébé." *("Not my baby.")* She kept saying. She said that we had to tell my dad—that he would help. She swore that they were going to take care of everything… I still don't know exactly what Pasteur Ben told them. But the next Sunday after service, my dad went into this long meeting with the rest of the church staff, and he was put on a temporary leave of his pastoral duties. "To give him time to focus on being a pastor in his own home." He said something about raising a daughter who is a liar and a temptress. I guess when it was the word of a sixteen-year-old girl against a man of God with a dead wife—there was no debating. My dad watched me come into this world, he raised me, but he still believed Pasteur Ben over me. And obviously everyone noticed, that all of a sudden my dad isn't preaching anymore, and Pasteur Ben is fully in charge and—next thing I know, there's all these rumours about me. That I threw myself on a disciple of God and lied about it and said he forced himself on me when he turned me down. Everyone was saying that I was a liar, a whore, a Jezebel living in the house of the pastor. Every Sunday, I had to sit in the front row knowing the entire congregation is talking about me. About our family. And that was just at church. At home, my parents just never talked about it again. I wanted to bring it up, but I didn't even know how. We just pretended like everything was okay. But it wasn't even good pretending. It just got so quiet all the time. I couldn't even defend myself to people. I wouldn't even know where to begin. So I just stayed quiet and hoped the rumours would disappear. It probably made more people think it was true. I don't know.

DIVINE: So that's why tonight… with Sarah? *(BIEN-AIMÉ nods.)* It's really messed up that people think that about you. That anyone would believe—

BIEN-AIMÉ: "Do not put your trust in princes, in human beings / who cannot save."

DIVINE: "Who cannot save." Did you ever tell Eric?

BIEN-AIMÉ: I had to, we were already dating before everything started. I think for a bit he believed me, but then he started to change… Said he needed space…

DIVINE: It shouldn't be like this, we're supposed to be Christians and love each other as God loves—I…I'm really sorry.

BIEN-AIMÉ: I know. Like I said: people suck. I'm really sorry I lied to you.

DIVINE: Don't be, I get it—I mean, I don't get it, but… So what do we do?

BIEN-AIMÉ: There's nothing to do, Divine, it is what it is.

BIEN-AIMÉ drinks the wine.

DIVINE: Maybe we shouldn't stay here. We can go hang out at my house or something? All these people coming to this youth group night, they've been so mean to you.

BIEN-AIMÉ: I'm over it. I don't care what these people think anymore. I'm good. And I have you.

DIVINE: You sure?

BIEN-AIMÉ: Yes! I'm going to show you how Christian girls party.

BIEN-AIMÉ takes another generous sip of wine; she offers some to DIVINE and gets up triumphantly.

DIVINE: Ugh, I don't know how you like this stuff. That's why I always take the grape juice at communion.

BIEN-AIMÉ: Okay, come on, get up. We're gonna go back down there. Drink a little, sweep our bullshit under the rug and have some fun tonight with those girls.

DIVINE: You slapped Sarah in the face. Hard.

BIEN-AIMÉ: I did, didn't I?

DIVINE: I think her cheek started to turn red.

BIEN-AIMÉ: Oh, stop it.

DIVINE: I'm telling you. Her skull was shaking like one of those bobblehead dolls.

BIEN-AIMÉ: You Africans love to exaggerate. Shit, I owe her an apology, don't I?

They collect themselves and their bottle of wine, which is nearly done, and head back into the church basement to join the other girls. SARAH and GRACE are playing music and getting ready, sipping Truth Juice from plastic cups. There is a small beat as everyone susses out the energy in the space. GRACE gives SARAH a nudge. SARAH gets up and pours BIEN-AIMÉ a cup of Truth Juice as a peace offering. She takes it. The two girls go into a corner to discuss privately. GRACE grabs DIVINE and brings her to the table.

GRACE: What do you feel about tequila?

DIVINE: I have no feelings about tequila. Never had it.

GRACE: You are losing your tequila virginity today.

DIVINE: I don't know…

GRACE: Come on. After all these nonsenses… tequila only makes it better.

DIVINE: I don't know…

GRACE: Come on now. Don't be the boring blanket!

DIVINE: Okay...okay, fine. I'll try.

GRACE giddily pours two hefty shots of tequila and hands DIVINE a lemon slice.

GRACE: Santé!

They toast and take the shots. DIVINE is disgusted by the tequila. She makes retching sounds and freaks out.

Lemon! Lemon!

DIVINE puts the entire lemon slice in her mouth. After a few seconds spits it out.

DIVINE: That didn't help. Lemons are terrible too.

She grabs a cup and fills it with Truth Juice and chugs it down.

GRACE: Eh eh, slowly! Slowly!

DIVINE: Ugh, that sucked.

GRACE: Tequila will be your best friend by the end of the night.

DIVINE: I doubt it.

SARAH and BIEN-AIMÉ do a pinky promise and come back to join the other girls.

SARAH: We're doing a shot!

DIVINE: No way.

SARAH: Yes, for forgiveness!

GRACE: Yes! Forgiving seventy times seventy-seven times seven.... seven times…

BIEN-AIMÉ: Just do one more shot with us Divine, for me. Please.

DIVINE: Fine, one more. Just one.

They toast "Cheers!" and take a shot. DIVINE gags less this time. The girls are all tipsy at this point. As time passes we see glimpses of them continuously getting ready as the music is blasting: occasional dance breaks; all of them helping DIVINE pick an outfit and fix her makeup; GRACE attempting to get SARAH to wear a dress to no avail; BIEN-AIMÉ checking herself out; DIVINE shyly appreciating her newly discovered fufu butt. Every now and then they take more shots. This transitions into the party in the sanctuary. The music swells. BIEN-AIMÉ grabs DIVINE by the hand and drags her into the church basement to regroup.

DIVINE: Are you having fun?

BIEN-AIMÉ: Why is Eric talking to that bitch Joelle Wabantu?

DIVINE: Uh…

BIEN-AIMÉ: She is dumb as rocks. Literally the definition of fufu for brains.

DIVINE: You should say something.

BIEN-AIMÉ: To who?

DIVINE: Eric!

BIEN-AIMÉ: No. I don't want to look like the desperate ex-girlfriend…again.

DIVINE: But maybe if you explain—

BIEN-AIMÉ: I'm done explaining myself—

DIVINE: But you guys loved each other. That doesn't just "poof" disappear after—

BIEN-AIMÉ: Just drop it. Let's go find Grace and Sarah, we still have that bet about getting a kiss tonight.

DIVINE: God help me.

BIEN-AIMÉ: He is a God of miracles.

They go back into the party. GRACE and SARAH break off on their own.

GRACE: You have to stop showing your behind like that!

SARAH: Ah, you're boring.

GRACE: No, I'm sane.

SARAH: You're jealous because I am going to get a kiss before you tonight.

GRACE: People are going to think you're crazy.

SARAH: Who cares what people think?

GRACE: Papa!

SARAH: He doesn't care about me anyway.

GRACE: He does, he's just—

SARAH: Whatever. You need to get a kiss tonight too. Why aren't you going after David?

GRACE: He won't stop hanging out with our brother. How am I supposed to kiss him then!

SARAH: You called him our brother again!

GRACE: Because he is.

SARAH: Yeah, but you never say that… it's as if he and Papa only belong to you…

GRACE: I'm sorry, okay? But I don't want to talk about these things now. I just want to get a kiss. I have been denied affection for too long. My lips are ready to come out of retirement!

SARAH: Okay, I know—I just…

GRACE: Maybe you can distract our brother so I can jump David and—

SARAH: I just—I want to explain to you…

GRACE: Ah, explanations are boring. I want to party! Let's just party!

DIVINE and BIEN-AIMÉ burst into their space, filling it with chaos and music.

DIVINE: WE'VE BEEN LOOKING FOR YOU!

GRACE: Eh eh, why is she screaming?

DIVINE: SORRY—sorry. There's a lot of music and loud people.

SARAH: It's called a party.

DIVINE: It was supposed to be a night of worship and fellowship.

BIEN-AIMÉ: We're fellowshipping right now.

GRACE: Yes, and I want to fellowship all on David's—

DIVINE: Whoa, okay!

GRACE: What? I was only going to say body.

SARAH: That's not much better.

Sound of something crashing or breaking. DIVINE begins to stress.

DIVINE: What was that?

BIEN-AIMÉ: Relax...

DIVINE: Have you seen how many people are in here? This is not just the other young people from our church.

BIEN-AIMÉ: Everyone is welcome in the house of God.

DIVINE: But I asked Pasteur Ben for this. I have the keys. This whole night is my responsibility—

BIEN-AIMÉ: Shhh!

BIEN-AIMÉ puts her arm around DIVINE.

From now on, these lips are only for drinking alcohol or for kissing boys. No more stressing out.

SARAH hands over her cup and they make DIVINE drink it, quickly.

SARAH: If you stress, you drink. If we catch you stressing, you drink double.

BIEN-AIMÉ: Still stressed?

DIVINE nods.

Drink up then.

SARAH and GRACE rush back into the party. BIEN-AIMÉ begins to go up the stairs but stops to look back at DIVINE.

Just have fun tonight. I promise, you'll be okay.

BIEN-AIMÉ exits back into the party.

DIVINE is left alone. She takes another drink and heads back into the party. Things are in full swing. The party swallows DIVINE. Somewhere between having fun and anxiety, she finds herself on a makeshift dance floor in the sanctuary. She bumps into SARAH.

DIVINE: I need tequila!

SARAH: Yes!

They scurry into the church basement to take tequila shots.

DIVINE: You should be nicer to her.

SARAH: I know, but we have a complicated thing because we were raised separately—and she always takes super long in the shower—

DIVINE: What? No. I'm talking about Bien-Aimé.

SARAH: Oh. We made peace.

DIVINE: Tonight, yes. But you better keep it. You don't know the full picture. She deserves better than what she's gotten… from you, her parents, Eric…

SARAH: What picture, Mundele?

DIVINE: I'm gonna make sure!

SARAH: Of what?

DIVINE takes her tequila shot, grabs a lemon slice and rushes back into the party.

DIVINE: We are the body of Christ!

SARAH: Who?!

SARAH takes her shot, pours herself another and heads back into the mix of the party. She gets caught up in the swing of the party, she is feeling free. We see her wave at someone, and she is beckoned over. SARAH follows them into a dark corner. The party rages on, BIEN-AIMÉ is searching through the sea of people for DIVINE.

BIEN-AIMÉ: Divine?

No answer, just music.

Divine?

BIEN-AIMÉ exits continuing her search. Moments later SARAH re-emerges from her dark corner, visibly shaken.

SARAH: Merde. Merde. Merde. *(Shit. Shit. Shit.)*

She pours herself another tequila shot, she downs it quickly. She is suddenly pulled away by BIEN-AIMÉ.

BIEN-AIMÉ: Why is Patricia Tambwe saying you licked her face?

SARAH: What?!

BIEN-AIMÉ: The correct response is "I didn't"…

SARAH: I—That's not what happened.

BIEN-AIMÉ: No one cares about the truth if the lie makes a better story.

SARAH: How many people has she told already?

BIEN-AIMÉ: That girl has such a big mouth, she's always spreading bullshit. Big time songi songi. No one can even take her seriously.

SARAH: Right. Yeah. Songi songi. She's a vicious liar. I would never—

BIEN-AIMÉ: Whatever happened, maybe it's worth telling your version of the truth? At least to Grace before / she finds out—

SARAH: Oh Jesus. Grace… Oh GOD. Antoine. My brother is here / too what if he—

BIEN-AIMÉ: You need to calm down, let's take a shot.

SARAH: Bien-Aimé, please don't say anything to—

BIEN-AIMÉ mimes zipping her lips. Pours two shots for them.

BIEN-AIMÉ: Come on!

SARAH: Oh, God…

BIEN-AIMÉ: Don't be a baby.

They take the shots.

SARAH: Ah, all this for the stupid competition.

BIEN-AIMÉ: Oh, yeah. I won, by the way.

SARAH: Déjà? *(Already?)*

BIEN-AIMÉ: Where are the others?

SARAH: I don't know. Who did you kiss?

BIEN-AIMÉ: Why does it matter? I won.

SARAH: You lie. If you won, you would say.

BIEN-AIMÉ: Where's Grace and Divine?

SARAH: Didn't I just say I don't know? Tell me who you kissed if it's real.

BIEN-AIMÉ: I….

SARAH: Fine, bye, liar.

BIEN-AIMÉ: I'm not a liar.

SARAH: So then?

BIEN-AIMÉ: ...David...

SARAH: David Lavoie-Bilolo?!

BIEN-AIMÉ: ...Yes.

SARAH: Ohhhh... wow. Grace is going to kill you!

BIEN-AIMÉ: I... I need to find Divine.

SARAH: She is VERY drunk.

BIEN-AIMÉ: For real?

SARAH: Yes! She's been taking sips out of other people's cups when they're not looking and sneaking off for tequila shots all night.

BIEN-AIMÉ Shit, at least she's having fun.

SARAH: Yeah, until she throws up or blacks out.

BIEN-AIMÉ: If you find her, let me know. And don't tell Grace— that the game is over. Please.

SARAH mimes her lips being zipped as she pours herself another shot. BIEN-AIMÉ takes off. The party is still in full swing. GRACE is searching for SARAH, finds her and whisks her off into the church basement

GRACE: Jesus, God in heaven. What is wrong with our family?

SARAH: Patricia Tambwe is a liar!

GRACE: Huh?

SARAH: Uh... I—wait, what are you talking about?

GRACE: I need Jesus to forgive me.

SARAH: What did you do!

GRACE: I let David… see my womanhood.

SARAH: Menteuse! *(Liar!)*

GRACE: Je te jure! *(I swear!)*

SARAH: Wow, he's been busy tonight.

GRACE: What do you mean?

SARAH: Shit.

GRACE: Sarah. What do you mean?

Beat.

SARAH: … he also kissed someone else tonight…

GRACE: You kissed David—?!

SARAH: NO! Not me! … Bien-Aimé.

GRACE: That bitch! That cow! Can never keep her nasty hands off someone else's man. I hope what they're saying about Divine and Eric is true. Bien-Aimé deserves a taste of her own pill.

SARAH: What are they saying about Divine and Eric?

GRACE: I didn't see, but Joelle Wabantu said she saw Divine sitting on Eric Mwanza's lap in Pasteur Ben's office. Everyone is talking about it.

SARAH: No… she wouldn't do that.

GRACE: Joelle said Divine was throwing herself at him. She called her desperate.

SARAH: Divine doesn't even know how to flirt.

GRACE: Exact. The tequila has her coming on strong.

SARAH: I mean, Eric Mwanza is really fine.

GRACE: Mhm, temptation and tequila got her. When Bien-Aimé learns of this, she'll see how she makes everyone else feel.

SARAH: Eh… maybe she doesn't need to find out.

GRACE: ….

SARAH: Grace! Don't tell her.

GRACE: Wait, why did you bring up Patricia Tambwe before?

SARAH: When?

GRACE: Just now.

SARAH: No…. I don't think I did.

GRACE: Sarah!

SARAH: Grace?

GRACE: Ah, enough games.

Beat.

SARAH: I think I want to kiss a girl.

GRACE: Okay, Katy Perry.

SARAH: I'm serious.

GRACE: Serious serious?

SARAH: Serious serious.

GRACE: Like…? Like, you like… Seriously?

SARAH: Yeah? I—I don't really know but… But I think so.

GRACE: Wow…

SARAH: …That's why I asked my mom to send me to Canada with Papa.

GRACE: Oh.

SARAH: I didn't want to mess up your life. Or your family. I don't think I could have stayed in Congo if…

Beat.

GRACE: Then Papa can't know.

SARAH: I know…

GRACE grabs SARAH's hand affectionately.

GRACE: Let's take a shot, sister. I want to dance.

They take another shot. GRACE grabs SARAH by the hand and pulls her back into the party. They twerk. The party shows no signs of stopping. BIEN-AIMÉ is searching through the sea of people for DIVINE.

BIEN-AIMÉ: Have you seen Divine?

No answer, just music.

Divine?

No answer, just music.

Divine?

SARAH and GRACE rush in.

Have you seen Divine?

SARAH: No, but we have to go.

BIEN-AIMÉ: What? Why?

SARAH: Someone said they saw Pasteur Ben's car pull up in front.

BIEN-AIMÉ: What?!

GRACE: Are you even listening?

SARAH: The party is over, we have to go.

BIEN-AIMÉ: Where's Divine?

SARAH: I don't know. But if the pastor discovers you here—

BIEN-AIMÉ: Shit. Shit. Shit.

GRACE: Divine will be okay. She—

BIEN-AIMÉ: She won't! Pasteur Ben gave her the keys, she—

GRACE: We are going. It's up to you to come or not.

BIEN-AIMÉ: ... Fuck. I—Fine! There's the emergency exit through the church basement. Let's go!

The girls scramble to get into the church basement unseen. Slight chaos as the party goers begin rushing to leave. The party begins to dissipate. GRACE, SARAH and BIEN-AIMÉ scoop up what they can from the church basement and escape into the night.

The music has stopped. The rest of the church remains silent. A door is heard opening and closing. The sound of footsteps in the distance.

DIVINE emerges from Pasteur Ben's office. She is barefoot, dishevelled, fighting to stand up straight. Someone is behind her. Before we can see his face—the lights fade.

Scene Six

Two days after the party. SARAH and GRACE walk into the church. The lights are on, but no one else is there. It is still quite messy.

GRACE: Why are we the first ones here?

SARAH: Divine is always the—I guess she probably doesn't have the keys anymore… It's a good thing Papa Thomas was here to open the door for us.

GRACE: Thank God for him and his bald head.

SARAH: I can't believe they cancelled the service today.

GRACE: Eh eh, look at what they did to God's house. There's no way they could have had a proper service in this mess.

SARAH: Grace… I feel a little bad…

GRACE: What for?

SARAH: Everything—nothing, I don't know…

GRACE: If you don't know then be quiet and get a broom.

SARAH: You don't feel bad?

GRACE: For what? Going to a youth group night? Coming to church for prayer on a Friday night and then getting pressured into a party?

SARAH: But that's not what—

GRACE: Ah ah ah, it's what we told Papa and that's what he told Pasteur Ben so…

SARAH: …so?

GRACE: So, that's what happened.

SARAH: But—

GRACE: But nothing. You don't know Papa's wrath yet. I don't want to be grounded until my wedding day. Stick to the story.

SARAH: Okay...

GRACE: Have you talked to your best friend Bien-Aimé since Friday night?

SARAH: She's not my— No. I have not. Have you?

GRACE: Have I? Please.

SARAH: I don't know.

GRACE: She's a bitch. I have nothing to say to her besides that.

They clean in silence. BIEN-AIMÉ walks in.

BIEN-AIMÉ: Rare to walk into a room with the two of you in it and have silence.

She laughs, they don't.

My parents were so mad I was at the party, they threatened to ship me back to Congo.

More silence.

What's going on?

GRACE: What do you mean?

BIEN-AIMÉ: We ran out of here Friday night, left Divine behind, and now no one is talking to me.

SARAH: Did you want to stay and get caught by Pasteur Ben?

BIEN-AIMÉ: Obviously not, but—

GRACE: So then?

BIEN-AIMÉ: I'm just trying to understand—

GRACE: Did you hook up with David on Friday?

BIEN-AIMÉ: Huh?

GRACE: Did you?

SARAH: Grace…

GRACE: No! Let her answer for herself.

BIEN-AIMÉ: You told her—

GRACE: Of course she did! She's my sister.

SARAH: I—

GRACE: Shhh. *(To BIEN-AIMÉ.)* So?

BIEN-AIMÉ: I'm not proud of it, but yes. We hooked up. I was drunk. I shouldn't have. I didn't realize what I was doing.

GRACE: OH! Were you blindfolded? Were you held at gunpoint?

BIEN-AIMÉ No… but, there was tequila and wine—

SARAH: Truth juice…

BIEN-AIMÉ: Yeah! We had truth juice too!

SARAH: No, tell her the truth.

Beat.

BIEN-AIMÉ: Fine. I messed up, okay? Pardonne-moi *(forgive me)*—he wasn't worth it. He's not even that good of a kisser. Too much tongue.

GRACE: I like tongue!

BIEN-AIMÉ: Okay! So you can kiss him!

GRACE: You think I want your sad seconds?! Is that it, Bien-Aimé? We are all supposed to live in your shadow? Just always trying to please you or not piss you off so we don't get slapped?

BIEN-AIMÉ: No! I—I wasn't trying to—it was an accident. I mean, not an accident but I didn't think—

GRACE: No, you don't think. You never think. You just do. I have been such a good friend to you since I came to Canada. I never did anything to you, and this is how you repay me?

BIEN-AIMÉ: No! It's not—Grace, I—

GRACE: No one ever thinks about me and my feelings. I'm so tired of it. Everyone just doing what they want and never thinking about Grace. Grace can't have anything. Not the boy she likes, not her own cellphone, not even her own bedroom.

SARAH: Wait—are you mad at me too?

GRACE: Yes—No. I don't know.

BIEN-AIMÉ: Okay. I get it. But if you're mad at Sarah, that's separate from me.

GRACE: Can you just say you're sorry!

BIEN-AIMÉ: I did! Sarah, I just said it, right? You heard me!

SARAH: I—I don't...

BIEN-AIMÉ: Fine. I'm sorry! Okay? Sorry.

GRACE: Incroyable. *(Unbelievable.)* Sorry for what?

BIEN-AIMÉ: Sorry for kissing David on Friday. Sorry for not telling you about it. Sorry for being a bitch, I guess!

GRACE: That's it?

BIEN-AIMÉ: ...Yes?

GRACE: Joelle Wabantu and Patricia Tambwe sent a text to everyone saying you told David that you are in love with him. And that you planned this whole party just to get with him!

BIEN-AIMÉ: What?!

SARAH: That's what they said. That you wanted to get back at Eric Mwanza.

BIEN-AIMÉ: That literally makes no sense. We just kissed. That's it.

GRACE: Can you just admit it? I am quite tired of your lies.

BIEN-AIMÉ: I'm not lying. You yourself said that Patricia was a liar—

SARAH: That was different.

BIEN-AIMÉ: How is it different? If she lied about you, she could lie about me!

SARAH: Bien-Aimé, come on... you have a history of—

BIEN-AIMÉ: Of what?

SARAH: Of lying. About Eric, about Pasteur Ben...

BIEN-AIMÉ: I never said anything to you about Pasteur Ben.

GRACE: Ugh… The whole church knows! You tried to get Pasteur Ben to sleep with you! He protected you and didn't tell your parents, but then you lied and told them he tried to force himself on you. You tried to ruin his life.

SARAH: I even heard you told people you were carrying his child.

GRACE: And then you claim that you wouldn't have sex with Eric, but he said you did—the whole time you were dating. So why did you guys really break up?

BIEN-AIMÉ What? No, Eric is a liar and—

SARAH: So everyone is a liar but you?

BIEN-AIMÉ: I can explain—if you just let me—

GRACE: Have you ever told us the truth about anything?

SARAH: We're trying to be your friends, but it's really hard when you always lie, Bien-Aimé.

GRACE: Is that even your real name?

BIEN-AIMÉ: Yes / of course, I—

SARAH: We have tried to give you a chance even after what everyone else at church says about you, but—

GRACE: We always have your back! Always! And for what? Hmph. We should have left you here on Friday—

GRACE is overcome with emotion, SARAH comforts her. DIVINE enters, carrying more cleaning products.

BIEN-AIMÉ: Divine. You're okay?

DIVINE: I guess. But I am never drinking again. My body hates me, everything hurts and—wait, what's going on?

BIEN-AIMÉ: Nothing, it's—

GRACE: Nothing? Nothing?!

SARAH: Shhhh…

DIVINE: Are you okay?

BIEN-AIMÉ: Not really, but we—

GRACE: What happened on Friday?

DIVINE: I—I don't know. That's what I want to ask you guys!

GRACE: Come on now.

DIVINE: Seriously, I barely remember anything! I don't even remember getting home. My parents took my phone away after the party— I've been dying to finally talk to you all and find out what happened.

SARAH: Divine… You… and Eric…

DIVINE: Me and Eric…what?

GRACE: In Pasteur Ben's office.

DIVINE: Pasteur Ben's office…? *(She tries to recall.)* Oh my gosh, yeah. Right, yes! I went to talk to him. About Bien-Aimé. I wanted to fix things between them.

GRACE: You had sex with him.

DIVINE: Se— What? Is that supposed to be a joke?

SARAH: Divine…

DIVINE laughs.

DIVINE: That's literally impossible!

GRACE: They're both liars. They deserve each other.

DIVINE: What are you even talking about?

SARAH pulls out her cellphone and shows BIEN-AIMÉ and DIVINE a photo.

SARAH: This…

DIVINE: Who…? Who is that?

BIEN-AIMÉ: Oh my God…

SARAH: It's you and Eric Mwanza being… having…

DIVINE: This is the biggest songi songi I have ever—

GRACE: It's real. Joelle took the photo herself.

DIVINE: A photo… of… of what? Of who?

GRACE: It's you and Eric—

DIVINE: That can't be me…. No, that's not—

BIEN-AIMÉ: That's the dress I lent you for the party…

DIVINE: There's no way… No. No. That doesn't make any sense.

BIEN-AIMÉ: You wouldn't—

DIVINE: I didn't.

GRACE: You did!

DIVINE: It's impossible. I wouldn't—ever—

GRACE: It's right there! On the phone!

SARAH: This is too much.

DIVINE: I don't understand what's happening. Why would— What is going on?

GRACE: Not even an excuse!

DIVINE: Because— No. *(She fights to recall.)* I went to talk to him. I did… to fix it. For Bien-Aimé, I wanted to fix it, but… but I don't remember any of—of whatever is in that—that picture or—

GRACE: So what is it, photoshop? A secret twin? You had Eric alone so you tried your chance with him. Enough with the lies!

DIVINE: I'm not lying, I don't lie. I—I don't remember what happened, but I know that I would never— *(She notices BIEN-AIMÉ.)* Bien-Aimé…I promise. It's not what it looks like. I promise.

GRACE: It looks like you are enjoying yourself. Hmph, look at that smile, your arms around his neck—

SARAH: C'est assez. *(Enough.)*

DIVINE: I didn't… Bien-Aimé… I've.. I've never even kissed a boy. Why would I ever do that—especially to you—please.

GRACE: You pretend to be innocent and all this, but it is fake. Just admit it.

GRACE grabs the phone from SARAH's hand and shoves it in DIVINE's face.

Look at what kind of friend you are.

SARAH: Stop, Grace!

DIVINE stares at the photo, the realization washes over her.

DIVINE: It is me… But, I… I don't remember any of… I wouldn't. Bien-Aimé… I wouldn't do that to you. I wouldn't do that to me…I'm saving myself… I would never—I… I wouldn't… but…I don't remember. I don't remember.

A heavy silence hangs over them.

BIEN-AIMÉ understands.

BIEN-AIMÉ: You don't remember?

DIVINE: No. I don't, I … I remember going to find him—to talk about you…we were talking about you. I swear—but then… it's a blank… Did Eric— Did he—

BIEN-AIMÉ: It's okay. I believe you. If you don't remember, then it didn't happen.

DIVINE: But it's there. It's in the picture— He—

BIEN-AIMÉ: It didn't happen, Divine. Okay? It didn't happen. You're okay… You're gonna be okay. I promise.

DIVINE: How?

BIEN-AIMÉ: I—

BIEN-AIMÉ takes a breath. She gently lays her hands on DIVINE's shoulders and slowly begins to pray.

Heavenly Father...please wrap your loving arms around Divine. Fill her heart with courage and her mind with peace. Before you formed her in the womb, you knew her and you set her apart. God, you know who she is, and who she will become. Remind her of that. Remind her that she is never alone. Give her the strength to face the unknown with confidence, knowing that Your plans for her are good. Amen.

The lights slowly begin to fade.

You're gonna be okay.

BIEN-AIMÉ and DIVINE are latching on to each other. SARAH has moved away from GRACE. The church is messier than before.

End of play.